EARLY CHILDHOOD EDUCATI

Leslie R. Williams, Editor   **Millie Al**

ADVISORY BOARD: Barbara T. Bowman, Harriet K. Cuffaro, Stephanie Feeney, Doris Pronin Fromberg, Celia Genishi, Stacie G. Goffin,Dominic F. Gullo, Alice Sterling Honig, Elizabeth Jones, Gwen Morgan, David Weikart

Children with Special Needs: Lessons for Early Childhood Professionals
MARJORIE J. KOSTELNIK, ESTHER ONAGA, BARBARA ROHDE, & ALICE WHIREN

Can I Play Too? Including Children with Disabilities in Preschool Programs
SAMUEL L. ODOM, Ed.

Developing Constructivist Early Childhood Curriculum: Practical Principles and Activities
RHETA DeVRIES, BETTY ZAN, CAROLYN HILDE-BRANDT, REBECCA EDMIASTON, & CHRISTINA SALES

Outdoor Play: Teaching Strategies with Young Children
JANE PERRY

Embracing Identities in Early Childhood Education: Diversity and Possibilities
SUSAN GRIESHABER & GAILE S. CANNELLA, Eds.

Bambini: The Italian Approach to Infant/Toddler Care
LELLA GANDINI & CAROLYN POPE EDWARDS, Eds.

Educating and Caring for Very Young Children: The Infant/Toddler Curriculum
DORIS BERGEN, REBECCA REID, & LOUIS TORELLI

Young Investigators: The Project Approach in the Early Years
JUDY HARRIS HELM & LILIAN G. KATZ

Serious Players in the Primary Classroom: Empowering Children Through Active Learning Experiences, 2nd Edition
SELMA WASSERMANN

Telling a Different Story: Teaching and Literacy in an Urban Preschool
CATHERINE WILSON

Young Children Reinvent Arithmetic: Implications of Piaget's Theory, 2nd Edition
CONSTANCE KAMII

Supervision in Early Childhood Education: A Developmental Perspective, 2nd Edition
JOSEPH J. CARUSO & M. TEMPLE FAWCETT

The Early Childhood Curriculum: A Review of Current Research, 3rd Edition
CAROL SEEFELDT, Ed.

Leadership in Early Childhood: The Pathway to Professionalism, 2nd Edition
JILLIAN RODD

Inside a Head Start Center: Developing Policies from Practice
DEBORAH CEGLOWSKI

Uncommon Caring: Learning from Men Who Teach Young Children
JAMES R. KING

Teaching and Learning in a Diverse World: Multicultural Education for Young Children, 2nd Edition
PATRICIA G. RAMSEY

Windows on Learning: Documenting Young Children's Work
JUDY HARRIS HELM, SALLEE BENEKE, & KATHY STEINHEIMER

Bringing Reggio Emilia Home: An Innovative Approach to Early Childhood Education
LOUISE BOYD CADWELL

Major Trends and Issues in Early Childhood Education: Challenges, Controversies, and Insights
JOAN P. ISENBERG & MARY RENCK JALONGO, Eds.

Master Players: Learning from Children at Play
GRETCHEN REYNOLDS & ELIZABETH JONES

Understanding Young Children's Behavior: A Guide for Early Childhood Professionals
JILLIAN RODD

Understanding Quantitative and Qualitative Research in Early Childhood Education
WILLIAM L. GOODWIN & LAURA D. GOODWIN

Diversity in the Classroom: New Approaches to the Education of Young Children, 2nd Edition
FRANCES E. KENDALL

Developmentally Appropriate Practice in "Real Life"
CAROL ANNE WIEN

Quality in Family Child Care and Relative Care
SUSAN KONTOS, CAROLLEE HOWES, MARYBETH SHINN, & ELLEN GALINSKY

(Continued)

CHILDREN WITH SPECIAL NEEDS

Lessons for Early Childhood Professionals

MARJORIE J. KOSTELNIK
ESTHER ONAGA
BARBARA ROHDE
ALICE WHIREN

TEACHERS COLLEGE PRESS

Teachers College, Columbia University
New York and London

Published by Teachers College Press, 1234 Amsterdam Avenue, New York, NY 10027

Copyright © 2002 by Teachers College, Columbia University

All rights reserved. No part of this publication may be reproduced or transmitted in any form or by any means, electronic or mechanical, including photocopy, or any information storage and retrieval system, without permission from the publisher.

Publisher's note: All chapter opening illustrations by Barbara Rohde. Used with permission.

Library of Congress Cataloging-in-Publication Data

Children with special needs : lessons for early childhood professionals / Marjorie J. Kostelnik . . . [et al.]
    p. cm. — (Early childhood education series)
    Includes bibliographical references and index.
    ISBN 0-8077-4160-4 (cloth : alk. paper) — ISBN 0-8077-4159-0 (pbk. : alk. paper)
    1. Handicapped children—Education (Early childhood)—United States—Case studies.   2. Early childhood education—United States—Case studies.   I. Kostelnik, Marjorie J.   II. Early childhood education series (Teachers College Press)
    LC4019.3 .C45 2001
    371.9'0472—dc21   2001041574

ISBN 0-8077-4159-0 (paper)
ISBN 0-8077-4160-4 (cloth)

Printed on acid-free paper

Manufactured in the United States of America

09   08   07   06   05   04   03   02   8   7   6   5   4   3   2   1

Contents

Preface

When early childhood practitioners contemplate having a child with special needs in their class, they may wonder:

- I've never worked with a child in a wheelchair before. Where do I begin?
- I don't have a degree in special education. How can I help a child in my class who has a condition called Turner syndrome?
- I'm worried. What if Sam has a seizure in school? What should I do?

Over the years, we have sought ways to answer such queries by inviting families and teachers of children with special needs to talk with our university students about their experiences. The format for these talks is conversational; participants describe a child and the people and/or experiences they believe have supported or failed to support that child's development and learning. These conversations are very personal. They are rich in detail and useful information. Some are humorous, others are tearful, and still others are filled with indignation. None are dull. Long after students graduate, they tell us these conversations have had a powerful impact on their attitudes toward families and children with special needs. They report that lessons gleaned remain with them long after other more didactic information has faded. We are pleased to share some of these conversations with you.

The purpose of this text is to give you a personalized introduction to some young children (ages birth to 8 years) who have special needs, their families, and their teachers. This is not a comprehensive textbook on children with special needs or on special education. It is meant to shed light on these topics and to help you as an early childhood practitioner feel better equipped to meet the needs of all the children in your early childhood setting.

This book contains 11 chapters. The first chapter introduces you to a holistic, inclusive view of working with children who have special needs in early childhood classrooms. Chapters 2–10 each profile one child: Andrew, Rosie, Sara, Marcus, Irina, Sam, Brian, Daniel, and Katherine Mary. *

---

*The names of the children, their families, and their teachers have all been changed to maintain confidentiality. Certain details related to location or other identifying variables have been modified for the same purpose.

Viewed as a group, the children illustrate various special needs. The children also differ in age, gender, culture, family composition, access to socioeconomic resources, geographic location, and educational setting. There is diversity among the storytellers, too; some are parents, some are siblings, some are teachers. Some stories have happy outcomes, some are less positive, and some are ambiguous. Our goal was not to be exhaustive, but to highlight the diversity that characterizes early childhood education today. Each of the nine child profiles includes the following segments:

- A description of the child
- An edited transcript of an interview with a family member or early childhood professional describing essential facts and historical incidents in the child's life
- An epilogue describing the current status of the child
- Factual information about the special need illustrated in the profile
- Hints for success (teaching strategies useful in working with children with similar special needs as well as their typically developing peers)
- Discussion questions
- Resources for professionals and parents

The last chapter pulls together big ideas addressed in the children's profiles. It also prompts you to reflect on ways to apply relevant content in your professional role. The book ends with a case study readers may use to synthesize what they have learned. Guidelines for an IEP (Individualized Education Program) are also included as Appendixes A and B to clarify the formal process used to bridge home and formal group settings. Appendix A describes the educator's role in the IEP. A sample IEP is presented in Appendix B.

ACKNOWLEDGMENTS

For every child whose story is told here, many more were not included. We wish to thank all the family members and early childhood professionals who gave freely of their time and expertise to tell their stories and share their insights. In order to preserve confidentiality, we cannot identify any contributor by name. However, we deeply appreciate their willingness to talk with us. The resulting conversations make this volume rich with caring and wisdom.

CHAPTER 1

Starting the Conversation

Working with Children Who Have Special Needs

It was the last few beautiful days of summer before Joanne had to head back to the classroom to prepare for the new school year. She was looking forward to a few hours of relaxing in the sunshine when her telephone rang. It was her principal, not a person she expected to hear from. He apologized for bothering her while she was still on vacation, but he felt she might appreciate having this bit of information before starting school the following week. He said that a new family was moving into the district with a little girl named Tricia, who had autism. She had little language and had attended a pre-primary special education class the previous year. The plan was for Tricia to attend Joanne's morning kindergarten and then return to her pre-primary class in the afternoon. He said the parents wanted to meet with Joanne, and he assured her that he would do all he could to support her in working with Tricia.

Now, relaxing seemed secondary, and Joanne began to ponder about autism. She had never had a child with a disability like that in all of her 4 years of teaching kindergarten. The principal seemed to be supportive, which was comforting. But foremost in Joanne's mind was, "What do I need to do to make this child's experience a good one?" For Joanne, teaching kindergarten had been her life's dream; she liked being the person introducing school to all of the 5- and 6-year-olds who came into her classroom. It was exciting to see how children left at the end of the year with a positive impression about school and feeling good about themselves as learners. For now, though, Joanne was feeling a little bewildered about how to welcome Tricia into her class. She had so many questions about how Tricia would relate to the other children and to her as a teacher.

The first thing that came into her mind was Jeremy, her college roommate Anne's younger brother. Joanne had never met Jeremy, but her roommate had talked a lot about him and how his having autism affected their family. He could speak but had trouble connecting with people, as Joanne recalled. Those stories Anne had shared about Jeremy now seemed too sketchy to provide much information about autism. Then Joanne started to think about finding out all she could about Tricia from her parents and her pre-primary teacher. Next she would . . .

Scenarios like this are played out by teachers in thousands of early childhood programs every day. Joanne is not alone in feeling uncertain and ambivalent about the prospect of having a child with special needs in her classroom. Currently, many early childhood educators have little or no training in special education, yet they face the challenge of working with children who have a variety of disabilities. Sometimes, as was true for Tricia, those disabilities have been formally identified early in the child's life. Such children have been observed or tested by specialists in the field and deemed eligible for special education services. Sometimes children's disabilities are just becoming evident. These youngsters arrive at their early childhood program undiagnosed but exhibiting behaviors and attributes that indicate they have special needs. In either case, practitioners like Joanne have a responsibility to support the development and learning of all the children in their settings, including those who have special needs.

The research and literature show that including children with special needs in early childhood programs results in positive development both for them and for their more typically developing peers (Allen & Schwartz, 2001; McDonnell & Hardman, 1988). Although early childhood educators have traditionally learned strategies for dealing with wide variations in children's development, they sometimes feel unprepared and unsure about how to work with children described as having special needs (Putnam, 1993). This chapter, and those that follow, are designed to help you feel more confident and knowledgeable as you strive to teach young children with disabilities in any of several different early childhood settings. Examples might include nursery schools, Head Start classrooms, state-funded preschool programs, child-care centers and homes, and elementary classrooms.

USING LABELS TO DESCRIBE CHILDREN WHO HAVE SPECIAL NEEDS

Early childhood educators are often taught not to label children. Yet it is common practice to use labels in describing the young child with special needs. This practice has benefits for children and their families, as well as negative aspects to be avoided.

Positive Uses of Disability Labels

Labels such as learning disability (LD), pervasive developmental disorder not otherwise specified (PDD-NOS), and physical or otherwise handicapped impaired (POHI) make children eligible for special education services. (See Chapter 10 for the definitions of disabilities in federal law.) Labels also provide initial indicators about some of the typical services that children with certain disabilities might need. Labels offer a concrete way of describing some aspects of a child's development. This gives practitioners and family members direction as they search the literature or make contacts in the community in an effort to learn more about the child. Although labels are helpful in assisting children to get special education services and can be used to help adults gain information that might enlighten them on the subject matter, there are some pitfalls to relying too much on labels in thinking about and working with children who have special needs.

The Negative Aspects of Labels

Labels describe only one dimension of a child's development. They do not provide sufficient information about the whole child. Thus, a child who is described as having attention deficit/hyperactivity disorder (ADHD) is likely to be very active and find it challenging to concentrate in a busy classroom. However, the ADHD label does not tell us that that same child is a talented musician, runs fast, and likes poetry. Moreover, there are wide variations among children who can be described with the same label. For example, one child labeled as autistic may have the ability to express affection and care for another person, while another child designated by that same label may not demonstrate such behaviors. As is true for all children, those with special needs vary widely in their characteristics and abilities. If early childhood professionals rely too much on labels, they can be misled, make false assumptions, further stigmatize a child, inappropriately limit their expectations, or overlook a child's strengths.

One way to avoid these pitfalls is by adopting a "people first" approach to using special needs labels in relation to individual children. With this in mind, if Michael has a learning disability, we would say he is a child with LD, not that he is an LD child. This simple practice reminds us that Michael is first and foremost a child. He has a learning disability, but that is not all we need to know about him. A single label cannot sum him up. A second strategy is to get to know each child as an individual. Thus making a commitment to understand each child for his or her unique strengths, challenges, and attributes is the first step in learning how to work with children who have special needs.

LEARNING ABOUT CHILDREN WITH SPECIAL NEEDS

Seeing each child as a unique individual is the first step in getting to know any child, including those who have special needs. You might begin by creating a profile of the child based on your firsthand observations as well as information gleaned from the people in the child's life. Basic questions to ask yourself include:

- How does the child react to sensations?
- How does the child process information?
- How does the child approach problems, make plans, and take action?
- What is the child's level of emotional, social, and intellectual functioning?
- How does the child communicate with others?
- What sort of interaction patterns does the child exhibit in relation to peers and adults?
- What do you know about family patterns and routines?

By gathering information around questions like these, you will have substantial information for developing a relationship with the child and for meeting each child's unique educational needs (Greenspan, Wilder, & Simons, 1998). Such information will come through observing children, listening and talking with them, communicating with members of their family, and consulting with colleagues in the field.

Observing Children

Observing children as a way of getting to know them is extremely important for all children, but even more so when it comes to children with special needs. Such children may not have verbal facility or may exhibit behaviors related to their disability that are not readily apparent through conversation.

Observations begin with each child's physical characteristics. Physical appearance has an impact on how children feel about themselves and how others respond to them. What does the child look like? What is the child's approximate height and weight? How does the child carry himself or herself when moving? Does the child move quickly or slowly? If the child is not mobile, in what other ways might he or she move parts of the body?

Carefully observing children's language, social, and cognitive development is also useful. For instance, observations about the child's choice of activities, his or her ability to stay on task, and the manner in which the child plays with others yield valuable information that contributes to an overall picture of each youngster.

Listening to Children

Listening is another fruitful way of getting to know young children. While this may seem obvious, too often grown-ups are poor listeners, focused more on what they want to say than on what children wish to communicate. In fact, there is evidence that adults are accurate listeners only about 25% of the time (Kostelnik, Whiren, Soderman, Stein, & Gregory, 2001). Thus true listening requires a deliberate effort to attend to what each child says and does not say. It involves paying attention to how a child constructs sentences and enunciates words. Listening also involves observing the child's ability to acknowledge the other person who is speaking and to engage in the give-and-take of conversation.

Through careful listening you can learn about children's interests as well as their likes and dislikes. Here, too, is an opportunity to learn about a child's assets. Identifying what the child is interested in, what he or she likes to do and excels in doing, provides rich information that makes this child distinctive from the others.

The affect in a child's voice provides data about the child's ability and inclination to express emotions. Is the tenor of the conversation flat? Is it one that conveys emotion—joy, anger, or excitability? Noting such variations gives you another perspective on each child.

Talking with Children

A child's style of communicating and interacting with you reveals more valuable information about him or her. Does the child respond to you when you initiate conversation? Does the child avoid speaking to you or to others? Does the child make eye contact? Through conversations with individual children, you will learn more about the level of language a child is able to use, the child's ability to provide descriptive responses, and the child's interests. If children are nonverbal, it is still important to talk with them. How do they respond to your words? What signs of communication might a child be exhibiting?

Extending Your Exploration

Observing, listening, and talking with children give you strategies for learning more about them and for discovering unique characteristics that might be obscured by general labels such as Down syndrome or a POHI designation. To gain a more accurate understanding of each child, it helps to remember that children develop and learn in context, not in isolation.

You can learn more fully about children by examining their behavior in multiple settings. For instance, in early childhood programs children can be observed in various situations—at the lunch table, on the playground, or in the classroom. Moreover, in the classroom you might observe children in the block area, at the water table, at the reading center, or at the computer. Youngsters can be observed playing alone, with a few children, or in whole-group activities. Observations might take place at different times of the day—during greeting time; while center activities are going on; during music, snack, or circle time. Thus early childhood programs include various circumstances in which children may exhibit different reactions and behaviors. You will get the most information by observing, listening, and talking to children in several of these settings rather than in just one.

Besides the early childhood program environment, children function in many additional settings in which they have contacts with a variety of people. Expanding your observations beyond the immediate surroundings of the classroom provides valuable information about children. Riding on the bus or in the van, visiting children's homes, and seeing children in their neighborhoods are all ways to extend your understanding of how particular children live and learn. Yet even when you have access to settings such as these, it is not possible to observe children in all the contexts in which they function. Instead, you may be able to ask questions of some of the important people in children's lives as a way to get to know children better.

Gaining Information from Family Members

Parents, siblings, and extended family are usually the richest source of information about a child with special needs. You might talk with family members at the program site and/or at their homes. Home visits provide an opportunity to talk with family members in surroundings that are most familiar to them. Although time-consuming, such visits can be a powerful means of demonstrating interest in the child and his or her family as well as your willingness to move out of the formal educational setting into a setting in which parents are in charge. Visiting children at home also enables you to meet other family members or persons living there and observe the child in context. Unfortunately, it is not always possible to conduct home visits. Time may not allow for this valuable contact, or families may feel uncomfortable having you come to their homes. If this is the case, it is still important to find other opportunities to talk with families about their children with special needs and to observe children interacting with members of their family.

As you talk and observe, there are certain things you will want to discover. What is the communication style of the family? How do the adults interact with the child, and how does the child interact with the adults? What role does the child play in the family? For example, being the youngest in a family of four is different from being an only child. Role expectations framed by cultural norms should also be heeded. Expectations of a young child in a traditional Japanese family are very different from expectations held for a child in a European American family. In every family, cultural values and beliefs influence how children are perceived and supported by family members.

Parents and family members are well equipped to tell you about communication strategies that work with the child and information about the child's likes and dislikes. They can also share, from their perspective, what challenges the child most. Here are some sample questions you might pose to get a broader perspective of how children function at home:

- What is the best way to get your child's attention?
- What kinds of things does your child like to do at home?

- What are your child's least favorite activities?
- With whom does your child spend a lot of time?
- What is something your child learned to do recently? How did he or she learn that?

Family members can also tell you how the child interacts with siblings and peers. Sample questions to ask include:

- How does your child relate to neighborhood children?
- Who does your child play with in the neighborhood?
- Who are your child's friends?
- What kinds of things does your child do with his or her friends/ siblings?
- What does your child say about friendships developed in the early childhood program?

Viewing the child with special needs as an individual is the first step in beginning to more fully understand the child. The child's individual profile can be developed by applying good observational skills, listening carefully to the child, and talking with the child. Additional information can be gleaned by examining the child through the lens of family, friends, peers, and other significant people in the child's life. Finally, cultural factors must be considered because they will influence how a child communicates, relates to others, and makes decisions. Thus understanding the child within the various contexts of his or her life is critical. The necessity of understanding the various contexts in which a child lives leads to the importance of collaborating with a variety of stakeholders who can potentially support the education and development of the special needs child.

BUILDING PARTNERSHIPS IN THE EDUCATION PROCESS

Communicating with Families

Family members are potentially valuable partners in the education process. Most important, they can offer information about the child overall and about the unique facets of the child's special needs. They can provide feedback about what they see at home; they can contribute strategies that might work best with their children; they can share ideas about valuable resources you might tap to support their child in the early childhood program. You will play an instrumental role in inviting and facilitating this partnership.

Family partnerships are fostered when you ask parents for their input, when you communicate what goes on in your classroom or child-care home, and when you provide opportunities for family participation in your program. In fact, the National Association of State Boards of Education (NASBE, 1988) recommends that all education programs serving children from birth through age 8 do the following things to promote positive home–program relations:

- Create an environment in which family members are valued as primary influences in their children's lives and as essential partners in the education of their children.
- Recognize that the self-esteem of parents/significant family members is integral to the development of the child and should be enhanced by the family's positive interaction with the program.
- Include family members in decision making about their own child and the overall early childhood program.
- Assure opportunities and access for family members to observe and volunteer in the classroom.
- Promote an exchange of information and ideas between family members and teachers that will benefit the child.
- Provide a gradual and supportive transition process from home to the early childhood setting for young children entering education and care programs for the first time.

Ideally, communication between you and the families of the children in your setting will be open and continuous. Developing agreed-upon processes for how information will flow back and forth is a good place to begin. The more communication flourishes, the more likely it is that greater consistency among settings will be achieved and that families and professionals will develop shared understandings and mutual goals.

Consulting with Special Educators

Sometimes a child may come into your setting already receiving special education services. For example, a speech therapist may be working with a child twice a week. Having some dialogue with that specialist will help you and the specialist more effectively assist the child in speech and language development. Yet another kind of connection might be with the pre-primary impaired (PPI) program, which is a kind of early childhood program dedicated to supporting special needs children. It is becoming increasingly common for children with special needs to spend part of their day in a setting devoted solely to children with special needs and part of the day in a program serving both typically developing children and those with special needs. Communicating with the teacher from the PPI program will help you to better understand that element of the child's world and to coordinate strategies from one setting to the other.

A child who is eligible for special education services by law is required to have an Individual Education Plan (IEP), which includes the child's educational goals and objectives and a plan by which the goals and objectives will be met. (See Appendixes A and B for more information about the development and contents of an IEP). You may be invited to participate in an IEP meeting, which is usually attended by parents, special educators, and anyone else the family chooses to invite and who will support developing a meaningful plan for the child. Sharing your knowledge about the child and your early childhood setting would be a valuable contribution to such a meeting.

YOUR ROLES IN THE LIVES OF YOUNG CHILDREN WITH SPECIAL NEEDS

Teachers and child-care providers play a key role in the lives of young children. What you say and do has the power to influence whether a child loves coming to the program or dreads it, how the child feels about learning, and how the child feels about himself or herself. Working with young children is an exciting prospect and a significant responsibility. It requires many talents and skills and, most of all, a keen appreciation for each child as a person with value and potential. This is particularly true for those children who have special needs. To carry out this endeavor successfully, you will assume each of the following roles.

Broker of Resources

Your role as a broker of resources includes both the child and his or her parents. For example, when Ahmed first entered the pre-primary program, his parents did not know about the lending library for children with special needs. His teacher was able to refer them to this resource, where they could access computer software that might help Ahmed learn some basic pre-primary concepts. Another example is the teacher referring a parent whose child has autism to a summer camp at which educational goals set for the year could continue to be supported over the summer.

Locksmith Opening Doors to Learning

Given the diversity of learning styles among children with special needs, you will be challenged to find the best method or methods to unlock the doors to learning for each child individually. Sometimes you will have to try multiple methods before finding one that works. Sometimes the motivation to assist learning and the sheer tenacity and belief that this is the right thing to do are what leads to success. For example, a new teacher in a second-grade class observed early in September that a child who was unable to read and could not tolerate much time with one-on-one reading lessons nonetheless loved to draw and tell stories about her drawings. Based on this, he decided to try having the child draw pictures to tell a story and then have her dictate an explanation of each picture. The child enjoyed her success in drawing an entire story and having her words written under the illustrations. She was able to listen to her story as it was read back to her and eventually she was able to recognize the words and associate letters with sounds.

Architect Designing Unique Opportunities for Learning

Children learn in many different ways (Gardner, 1999; Riding & Raynor, 1998). Some children learn best on their own through self-paced activities; others find relating to peers and collaborating most comfortable. Some children are highly dependent on learning through touch and movement; others rely more on visualizing; still others use language as their primary medium for learning. There are children who are adept at looking for patterns and relationships among objects and events, children who are more intrigued by rhythm and melody, and children who have a special affinity for observing and interacting with plants and animals. Whatever mode, or combination of modes, dominates their approach to learning, children are most likely to be successful when they have access to learning opportunities that match the modes they favor. Using a variety of strategies in your teaching is the easiest way to make sure children have such opportunities.

In addition, the innovative educational "architect" creates alternative learning experiences, adapts program structures, and modifies established routines to accommodate children's special needs. For example, one provider, who had a child with ADHD in her program, assigned an adult to sit next to the child to help him attend to and participate in group-time activities without disrupting others. The provider also allowed the child to move about in nondisruptive ways, once the story was over, if he showed signs of being unable to sit any longer with the group.

Bridge Builder Connecting the Child with Others

Early childhood settings are often the very first places where children begin interacting with peers. As a result, children learn some of their earliest lessons about relationships in such settings. This is especially important to families with children with disabilities who include the development of friendships among their goals (Turnbull & Ruef, 1997). In fact, there is strong evidence that early childhood educators can play an instrumental role in facilitating friendships between children with disabilities and children without disabilities (Turnbull, Pereira, & Bue-Banning, 2000).

Principles of friendship and communication that apply to children who have no disability also apply to children with special needs. Naturally, you must first consider children's developmental characteristics. Based on that, promoting friendships can be carried out using the following three-part framework (Schaffner & Buswell, 1992):

1. Find opportunities to bring children together.
2. Provide interpretations for children that will facilitate interaction, including acknowledging each child's strengths and commonalities among peers.
3. Make accommodations to support peer interaction and children's participation in peer-oriented activities.

Children are naturally curious about one another. It is not unusual for typically developing youngsters to notice that one or more of their peers have special needs. Early childhood professionals address such situations by answering children's questions matter-of-factly and honestly. They often include the child with special needs in such conversations, too. If a child with special needs is being teased or harassed by other children, early childhood educators stop the bullying behavior immediately. Afterward they strive to foster greater awareness and empathy among all children as a way to forge positive connections among peers.

Arbitrator of Conflicts

It is common in early childhood settings for children to become involved in conflicts around sharing materials and taking turns. When this happens, regardless of whether the children involved have special needs, teachers must help children develop the skills they will need to resolve conflicts peacefully. For example, Theresa, who has cerebral palsy, liked to be first in line. She wanted to be the leader of the group whenever a line was formed. One day Carl declared that he wanted the privilege of being first, which resulted in some shouting and pushing between the two children. Their teacher stepped in and stopped the hurtful behavior. Next, she mediated the conflict between the two children, helping them to work out a solution that satisfied them both. Later, the teacher took a few minutes at group time to talk to the class about taking turns, about being leaders, and about how each person in the class should have turns at being first. Children have a keen sense of equity, and this type of conversation underscored that all children have rights that must be honored.

Champion of Hope and Inspiration

Undoubtedly, there will be challenges in the journey of caring for and educating any child. However, children with special needs present unique challenges. Having a sense of hopefulness for and being able to convey a sense of hopefulness to children with special needs creates a sense of commitment and an expectation that produces growth.

Where can you go to generate this sense of hopefulness? Hope begins through observing the development of each child; every new development (although these may not appear at the same rate as would be true for a typically developing child) needs to be appreciated. It comes from "putting one foot in front of the other" and supporting little steps of growth and learning. Finally, it comes from developing a hopeful perspective.

> Hope works in these ways: it looks for the good in people instead of focusing on the worst; it discovers what can be done instead of grumbling about what cannot be accomplished; it regards problems, large and small, as opportunities; it pushes ahead when it would be easy to quit; "it lights the candle instead of cursing the darkness." (Anonymous)

The following chapters include a wide range of stories told by parents and practitioners about their own experiences with and the experiences children have had in early childhood settings. Their conversations cover many dimensions of the educational process and caring for young children. Each story offers insights and ideas you can use to include special needs children in your setting. We offer them as a resource to enhance your teaching and to provide some of the inspiration you will need to continue your work.

REFERENCES

Allen, K. E., & Schwartz, I. S. (2001). *The exceptional child: Inclusion in early childhood education* (4th ed.). Albany, NY: Delmar.

Gardner, H. (1999). *Disciplined mind.* New York: Basic Books.

Greenspan, S., Wilder, S., & Simons, R. (1998). *The child with special needs.* Reading, MA: Perseus.

Kostelnik, M., Whiren, A., Soderman, A., Stein, L., & Gregory, K. (2001). *Guiding children's social development* (4th ed.). Albany, NY: Delmar.

McDonnell, S., & Hardman, M. L. (1988). A synthesis of best practice guidelines for early childhood services. *Journal of the Division of Early Childhood Education, 12*(8), 328–391.

National Association of State Boards of Education (NASBE). (1988). *Right from the start.* Alexandria, VA: Author.

Putnam, J. W. (1993). *Cooperative learning and strategies for inclusion.* Baltimore: Brookes.

Riding, R. J., & Raynor, S. (1998). *Cognitive styles and learning strategies: Understanding style differences in learning and behavior.* London: Fulton.

Schaffner, C. B., & Buswell, B. E. (1992). *Connecting children: A guide to friendship facilitation for educators and families.* Colorado Springs, CO: PEAK Parents Center.

Turnbull, A. P., Pereira, L., & Bue-Banning, M. (2000). Early childhood educators as friendship facilitators. *Teaching exceptional children, 32*(5), 66–70.

Turnbull, A. P., & Ruef, M. B. (1997). Family perspectives on inclusive lifestyle issues for individuals with problem behavior. *Exceptional Children, 63*, 211–227.

C H A P T E R   2

Andrew
Absorbed with the Particulars

"Mr. Andrew"—that's what his family calls him. His mother shows us several photographs. "Oh, this is a solemn Andrew" (the 5-year-old in the picture looks past the camera—clear-eyed, round-cheeked, lips barely parted). "This is the more cool Andrew" (in this picture, Andrew, head tilted to one side, hair brushed back, looks straight ahead, sunglasses in hand). He is a handsome child . . . everyone says so. He loves video games, rock music, flashy new cars, and pretty girls. Andrew lives with his mother and 18-year-old sister (Aki) in a medium-sized midwestern town. Although he is now in the sixth grade, his formal education began in a preschool program for children with special needs.

ANDREW'S MOTHER TELLS HIS STORY

Every day is a new day with Andrew. Because of his autism, some small achievements have taken months, even years, to accomplish. On other days, you would think that maybe 6 months had passed between the night when we went to sleep and the morning when we woke up.

Andrew seems to be and always has been an independent person. I really never had to entertain him; he is always finding something to do.

The first thing I usually hear from people about Andrew is that he is so funny. In fact, he is the class clown. The other kids and teachers say, "He makes us laugh." So I think one of Andrew's assets is that people like to laugh and people are able to enjoy him as a person.

Andrew has certain typically autistic behaviors, like rocking when he gets anxious. Also, when he is excited he rocks back and forth. He was never involved in self-mutilation. Some children bang their heads until they bruise or bleed. He didn't do that, fortunately.

Andrew can get some very rigid ideas of how things should be. He would make an excellent quality-assurance person because he can look at something and say, "Oops, there is something wrong with that little piece of paper," or "That thing is chipped," or "Something is not in the proper order." He is quick to point out things that do not seem quite right.

You know, when I say Andrew has autism, people think of *Rainman*, the film starring Dustin Hoffman as a man who has autism and is also a savant [*a person who has exceptional skill in one particular arena such as music or mathematics skills in conjunction with extremely low ability in most other skill areas*].* That movie was a great thing for people with autism because the word is no longer such a mystery. But Andrew is certainly not a savant. I would have taken him to Vegas long ago if he had that capability (*she chuckles*), but he is not that.

Becoming Aware of Andrew's Special Needs

Andrew was born on April 19, and he had a perfect Apgar score [*a rating used to assess an infant's physical condition immediately after birth*]. He was a perfect baby. He was not like my daughter, who was colicky. He did not scream and cry. He was a joy.

When he was 1, I noticed that he often seemed like he was looking into outer space or something. But he was still a pleasant baby. By age 2, he was really oppositional. But, you know, 2-year-olds do say "no." However, this was an extreme kind of thing. He would get into bursts of crying

---

*Note: all italic text in brackets is commentary by the authors.

spells where his face would puff up and it was difficult for him to deal with any kind of change or anything that wasn't his way. His language was another sign that something was wrong. He was extremely developmentally delayed. I kept watching him. I was trained in special education. I thought that he might have autism because of his rocking and his echolalia. I suspected it and mentioned this to the pediatrician. He said, "Do you really believe that?" I said, "I hope he isn't." That's all I could say.

When Andrew was almost 3, my girlfriend from Arizona was visiting with her daughter, who is about the same age as Andrew. The children were in the backyard playing in an inflatable wading pool. The little girl was chattering away, but all Andrew could say was, "Jump into the water. Jump into the water." There was such a difference between the two children. My friend pulled me aside and said, "You know, I think it wouldn't hurt to have him tested." At that point I thought "yes," and I agreed.

Diagnosis

We went out of state to have him tested at a regional center for children with learning disabilities. We were assigned an audiologist, a speech therapist, a special educator, a developmental pediatrician, and, oh yes, three psychiatrists. There was a psychologist, too, who did all types of intelligence tests.

I can still remember the round-table meeting after 2 days of testing. They were all sitting around giving their reports. It was probably the most depressing day of my life. The best scores said he was mildly retarded, the worst said he was so developmentally delayed that he was clear off the scale. You think it couldn't be possible, but it is. The one good thing they told me was that he could hear and that he didn't have a hearing impairment. Then the psychiatrist put him into the developmentally disabled autism category. They indicated that this was a pervasive disorder; it wasn't something that was going to go away.

The pediatrician, who later became a good friend, wanted to do some further testing. She had a colleague, a biogeneticist, she wanted involved in this. She asked if Andrew could give another urine sample and a blood sample. The next call we got (a few months later) was that they would like to get a deep-tissue specimen, which would mean surgery. It was an outpatient procedure, but he would need a general anesthetic. I decided to do that, thinking we would find something that would be useful to him.

They sent the tissue samples to three or four labs around the country for different people to examine. They came back with a diagnosis of cytochrome oxidase deficiency. Another way to say it is mitochondrial impairment [*mitochondria are small granular bodies in human cells that function in certain phases of the metabolic process*]. Basically this diagnosis means that his cells do not produce enough energy and that is why his brain, which needs a lot of energy, is not functioning properly.

Usually, this is a progressive, fatal disorder. But, because Andrew has some mitochondria that are healthy, we are all hoping this won't be the case and that he will be fine.

I didn't want Andrew to be labeled. I was very much against the stigma and the label autistic. But if I wanted services, he wouldn't receive them without the label. So he has been officially categorized as having autism.

Interventions

Right away, we were told to consider behavior-modification strategies because that's one of the best ways to help children like this. This is something I have had training in, but I really have misgivings about using behavior modification as a total way of teaching people.

When he was 3, we started Andrew in a PPI [*pre-primary impaired*] class in the public schools. He went half-days in the mornings.

When he was 5, we got the mitochondrial diagnosis and were told to start vitamin therapy. So we got vitamin K and magnesium and B_6 vitamins combined. We started first with the B_6 magnesium and didn't see much difference in behavior; then we added K to it. When we added K—we were amazed that Andrew began to talk in full sentences. The behavior change was dramatic. It was this little yellow pill called vitamin K and he started talking, not really well, but a lot more than his "jump into the water" and two-word statements.

A specialist at the Autism Research Institute in California recommended that we also try DMG, which is another food supplement. I think they are using it in clinical trials in Israel with kids with autism. The self-report information from families is that it also helps to produce language. So we have him on that now.

Family Reactions

People in my family have had varying reactions to Andrew and his disability. My one sister's response was that she wanted us to put Andrew in a residential private setting. I was stunned by that. I would never have thought of sending him away.

My mother's response has been to pray. We're Buddhists. So we went to the Shingon temple and had the monk pray for Andrew. He said Andrew would be okay. Whatever "okay" meant, that was fine with my mom.

My other sister has a scientific point of view. She says whatever science says, that's the way it is. Her acceptance of Andrew is total. When she sees him, she says positive things like, "Oh, look at all the things he can do for himself." She is sort of a model for me in that respect.

It was hard for Andrew's dad to accept the fact that Andrew had a disability. It was tough for him—he wanted to fix Andrew. I think his father really cares about him, but he truly had difficulty with that part.

Andrew's sister, Aki, has always thought the world of him. When we were first working through Andrew's diagnosis, we had genetic counseling. We couldn't find any relatives that were like Andrew, so the doctor said he might have been the result of a mutation. When Aki heard that, she was about 8 years old. She said, "You mean Andrew is a Teenage Mutant Ninja Turtle?" And that was her understanding of who he is.

Aki has always been good with Andrew. She never tries to treat him like he has a disability. She argues with him. She is also protective of him and tells me the good things that happen to him at school.

[See Figure 2.1 for the important people, places, and activities in Andrew's life.]

Challenges

Andrew struggles through transitions. When he was 3 years old, leaving home and going into the school setting was extremely difficult. In the morning, teachers would have to come out to the car to get him because when I would try to take him into the building, he would grab onto my clothing and tear buttons off. By the time I got to work, I was a basket case. Once he was in school, he was fine. But it was getting from home to the school setting that was the real challenge.

For me to take Andrew shopping, I had to do a lot of pretalking before we'd go." In an hour we are going to the store. . . . In half-an-hour we are going to the store. "Only after all of that would he put his coat on and go with me. Going through a day's activities with somebody who is not able to transition into new settings was one of the toughest things we had to do with Andrew when he was little.

Another big challenge is when Andrew has an outburst in public. People can be very judgmental and quick to jump to negative conclusions. Because Andrew looks like a normal child, onlookers seldom understand his behavior in the context of the disorder he has. Instead, they see him as an undisciplined child and me as a lax or poor parent. For example, when Adrew was 8 years old we were on a flight to Florida. He was sitting next to me when it was announced that all tray tables should be in their upright position. Andrew decided he wanted the table

Figure 2.1. Andrew's world.

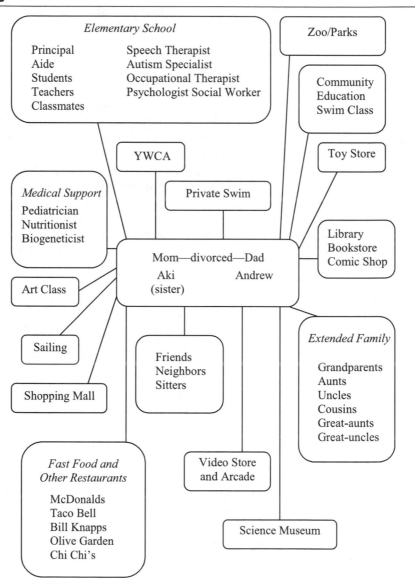

Elementary School

Principal   Speech Therapist
Aide   Autism Specialist
Students   Occupational Therapist
Teachers   Psychologist Social Worker
Classmates

Zoo/Parks

Community
Education
Swim Class

YWCA

Toy Store

Medical Support
Pediatrician
Nutritionist
Biogeneticist

Private Swim

Library
Bookstore
Comic Shop

Mom—divorced—Dad
Aki   Andrew
(sister)

Art Class

Sailing

Friends
Neighbors
Sitters

Extended Family

Grandparents
Aunts
Uncles
Cousins
Great-aunts
Great-uncles

Shopping Mall

Fast Food and
Other Restaurants

McDonalds
Taco Bell
Bill Knapps
Olive Garden
Chi Chi's

Video Store
and Arcade

Science Museum

down and was insistent about it. I simply said the table had to be up and began to stow it properly. Andrew became very upset and began to protest loudly. As I struggled to cope with the situation, the man in the seat across the aisle leaned over and said, "What that child needs is some strong discipline. You'll have to get a better handle on things if he's to grow up to live in a civilized society." I was so upset and embarrassed I didn't say a thing in response. We've had several similar episodes over the years. Although such incidents are hard on us, I continue to take Andrew into public settings. I think it's important for us to remain connected to the community we live in, not shut away from life just because of potentially embarrassing or awkward situations.

Milestones

When Andrew started in the PPI program at age 3, he was still not toilet-trained. His first PPI teacher toilet-trained him. That was wonderful and very practical. After that, he was able to go on the pre-primary bus and spend half-a-day at school. I'm not sure how much actual learning he was doing. He would be in the middle of the room with the other kids, but there wasn't much interaction of any sort. However, the fact that he was able to get out of the house, go to another setting, and participate even marginally was an okay beginning. We knew that when he went to elementary school he needed to have those abilities. So we kept him in the district's PPI program for 3 years. The last year, he also went to kindergarten at his regular neighborhood school for half-a-day.

Between the ages of 2 and 5, Andrew's language was minimal. He would throw huge temper tantrums, frequently. When the vitamin K came into his life, he began to communicate in words instead of actions, and that was a big breakthrough. The temper tantrums didn't happen as often or last as long.

The first day Andrew went to kindergarten, we all wanted to see how it would go. On the very first day, my mother was behind a bush, his father was looking on from another angle to the side, and I was walking him to the door. Andrew left me and walked into the building on his own and stayed with the teacher. It was like a miracle. I remember the principal came out to the sidewalk and said, "Now that wasn't bad at all." I said, "Dr. Steinmann, that wasn't bad, but there will be days when you will say, 'That wasn't so good either.' So be prepared for those days." We laughed, and that's how I remember the first day of kindergarten.

The school assigned Andrew an aide. He liked her but didn't like having an aide with him all the time. So in music class, around age 6 or 7, he told the aide to stay out of the room. "You stay here," he demanded.

She said, "I will stay in the hall if you listen to the teacher." And that went okay. Then one day he threw a tantrum. The teacher said, "Andrew, you have to leave; you cannot do that in class." He was sent out, and he never forgot it. After that he listened and he stayed with the group and he remained in music without an aide. That made him feel more grown-up and more like the other kids.

Feeling Part of the School Community

Andrew went to kindergarten in an elementary school where they had never had a child with autism before. The people were very pleasant, but I knew they were scared.

I remember them fondly because I think they were unsure of what to do and nobody had all the answers. But what they had was a belief that they could contribute or they could do something. I found it reassuring as a parent, to see that they were willing to try and learn from their mistakes. I never thought they should have all the answers. I just wanted them to care enough to try to figure it out and make the best of it.

In the first grade there was a significant incident when Andrew "mooned" the other children at recess and the principal talked to him. At that time, Andrew was able to communicate with a "yes" or "no," and we felt he understood what was being said to him. He had eye contact with her and understood that it was not appropriate behavior even though the other students thought it was funny. What was significant about this was not that Andrew stopped the behavior (although he did), but the fact that the principal took it upon herself to talk to him and then to the other students about their role in not encouraging Andrew to do things that were inappropriate. (She went to each class individually to discuss the matter). I thought it was really important for all the children, including Andrew, to have a sense of being responsible for their own behavior.

When Andrew was in the second grade, Aki came home one day very distraught because the school safeties had teased Andrew. So I went to the school. I didn't get to see the principal because she was unavailable, but I ran into Andrew's resource teacher. I said, "This is the situation and I'm concerned because I work and it is so convenient for him to walk home with his sister. However, if she continues to be upset because kids tease him, she is not going to want to do this. Plus, I don't want him to be teased." She said, "Tomorrow I am going to be on the path. I am going to walk with him and talk to them." And that happened. The problem totally stopped. She talked to the teacher in charge of the safeties, and they had a discussion. The swiftness of the response was unbelievable. The problem was solved. It has never occurred since.

Both of these situations show wisdom in how to build a sense of community in a school setting. Certain things were just not tolerated, and children knew they were accountable. The adults made clear that they were there to make sure people were treated with respect and that people were made to feel welcome. I think the whole community ethic was cultivated not only by the principal but by all the personnel in the school—they all contributed to it.

One other incident illustrates Andrew's inclusion in the school community. A group of thespians in our town have a contest where all the children write a story and submit it to a panel of teachers and children from the school. This panel selects 15 stories from all grade levels to send to the actors. The thespians select three of the stories to enact when they come to the school for an assembly. Unbeknownst to me or to Andrew, one of his stories, one about aliens, was submitted [see Figure 2.2]. Nobody knew who won until the thespians came. On that day, everybody was assembled in the gym, and the thespians acted out Andrew's story. It was a very simple story, but the students in his class were like cheerleaders. You could hear them. They were so happy he won. I thought this was really genuine. I had to be out of town that day, but they videotaped it for me so I could see it. I was stunned watching the video. The writer got to sit in the writer's chair and they were interviewed. Andrew was asked these questions and would answer, "yes," "no," "I don't know." But there he was in the writer's chair. His teacher and the class were absolutely ecstatic about it. They talked about it for days. I'm not sure Mr. Andrew thought it was great. He seemed nonplussed about it. His demeanor was not beaming and smiling and happy, but he was a significant student in his own little way. He had a role in the group, and that was encouraging.

Helpful Professionals

The willingness of professionals to not give up has meant a lot to Andrew and to me. The most helpful people in Andrew's life have been the ones who are able to problem-solve and who are flexible. They think "outside the box" because I don't think there are easy solutions to some of the situational things that cause Andrew to throw a tantrum or have difficulty to the point that you wonder how to possibly include him in a learning activity. Some professionals have come up with very creative solutions about how to help him learn. For example, if you were to talk to his kindergarten teacher, she could tell you about some pretty bad days when Andrew would be screaming out in the halls. At that age, his favorite activity was to pour sand. If he threw a tantrum, someone would take him out to the sandbox, and he would just pour sand until he calmed

Figure 2.2. Pages from Andrew's story about space aliens.

One day an alien was in space.

He came to Earth. He was sticking his tounge out.

The alien is not friendly

down, and then he would be brought back to the classroom. Sometimes I think he spent a lot of time in the sandbox pouring sand, but they were really willing to do things to accommodate him in that setting.

When Andrew went to first grade, he ran into a student teacher who was very overtly emotional in his demeanor. This teacher was able to express joy quite openly. Andrew really took to him. He talked about Andrew like he was a great person. The other kids got that kind of positive affect from him, and I swear, after that, it was easier for Andrew to connect with the other students.

This student teacher also believed in the whole-language approach, so he had the children write stories, draw them, and create books. And, by golly, Andrew drew a dinosaur book. We still have that book. Andrew couldn't write, so the teacher had Andrew dictate to him. I never thought that Andrew could be so much a part of a reading lesson. It was an affirming occasion.

I never had the school say to me, "Don't let him read comic books." Andrew loves comic books. In fact, they would reward him with comic books—Batman, Spiderman, and Garfield. They made sure they had reading material he would be engaged with. This was not the basal reader or anything like that, which he had no interest in reading. They really adapted to what motivated him.

Andrew hated going to speech. The reason, I think, was because it was a pull-out program in which he was all alone. He also knew he wasn't like the other kids. He wanted to be with the guys. There was a speech teacher at the school who problem-solved around that very effectively. Sometimes she would have his buddies come with him to the speech room, or she would do a group thing in class that would help all the children in language building. Andrew learns a lot from modeling, so she would use peers to model and they would play games. That was good.

Bad Times

Andrew had several speech teachers. The one that was least helpful was the one who was determined to teach Andrew to pronounce certain words according to her timetable. She had a list of words on his IEP [*Individual Education Plan*], and that was all she was interested in working on. [*See Appendixes A and B for information on an IEP.*] I would say, "If he fusses over a certain word, work on something else. There are so many other things you can teach him." No, she was determined to follow her schedule. It was a big waste of time.

Probably the most hurtful of my interactions with school happened while Andrew was first in the PPI program. I was a novice about being the parent of a child with a disability. Everything was new to me. I wasn't sure how he would survive in the school system. The PPI program was part of an early childhood center, with preschool and kindergarten only. There was an annual winter holiday program for parents. The children would be singing and doing small performances of some sort. A few days before the event, I got a letter saying, "You need not bring Andrew to this activity because I don't think he'd benefit from it." I couldn't believe the teacher would write a note like that. I remember feeling dumbfounded, hurt and weeping. I would be okay for a while, and then I would burst into tears. Usually if I am upset, I will call the person responsible for the problem and try to talk it out. I couldn't do that. I couldn't talk to her. I couldn't face her. I was a basket case. This went on for months. Finally, my daughter said, "Mom, just write her a letter." I wrote a letter, but I never mailed it. I was paralyzed, I think, by sadness and grave disappointment about how someone perceived my son. I used to volunteer in the program, but I didn't go back after that. The next year, there was a new PPI teacher, and Andrew had a great time with her.

Advice for Early Childhood Professionals

It is very important to get to know the child. Listen to parents and to other people who know the child and take in what they say. Really listening is critical.

Don't make quick judgments about the child based only on the behaviors that seem negative. That's just part of the child, and there are other parts of the child worth exploring.

Respond to parents of a child with special needs even if the child isn't in your room. There were a lot of teachers at Andrew's school who would come up to me and say specific things that happened to Andrew at school. A remark like "You know he likes to swing at recess" indicated to me that this teacher knew who he was.

Work with parents on how to teach the child. You have varying types of parents. Some parents want constant communication, others want much less. If the parent is willing, share your ideas. Also, listen to parents and get input about strategies that might work in the classroom. You don't have to do everything a parent tells you to do, but it helps if parents feel some degree of partnership in the whole process.

Epilogue

Andrew is 13 years old now and about 5 feet 5 inches tall. I'm amazed at how much he eats. I used to hear stories about boys eating a lot—they're true. He is a thin kid, but he's ravenous and goes through food at an unbelievable rate. He makes his own things in the microwave oven. He is very self-sufficient, and he will make pronouncements about what he likes and what he doesn't like. I think that he has become his own best advocate. He is also an advocate for his peers. The other day in sixth grade, the teacher said something hurtful to another child. Andrew stood up and said, "You shouldn't talk to him like that. You should be fired." The teacher was angry, but I felt good that Andrew has become aware of other people to that extent.

Andrew's world right now is filled with comic books, drawings, and listening to his CDs. His favorite things to do are to go to Aladdin's (a video game arcade in the community) and to the Capital City Comic Shop, where they all know him.

Although his ability to read and do math is at a first- or second-grade level, Andrew's knowledge of music trends and knowledge of what is cool for his age are developmentally there. So when you see an individual and you say, "yes, he has deficits or disabilities," you can't assume that is true across the board in everything he does. I had this stereotype about my son having a disability and thought he would not be interested in women, or music, or fancy cars, or nice clothes. But he is appreciative of all these things.

My dreams for Andrew's future are for him to have a good life and for him to continue to grow and develop and gain more skills that will enable him to have greater degrees of freedom. The most important thing is that he have happiness and joy and be surrounded by people who care about him.

Information for Educators About Autism

Andrew McDonald has been diagnosed with a form of autism. Autism is a lifelong developmental disability that is typically identified in the first 3 years of life. It is a neurological disorder affecting the brain and occurring in approximately 2 to 4 per 10,000 births. This condition is four times more common in boys than it is in girls (Autism Society, 1998). The precise cause of autism remains unknown. Although people once believed that it resulted from poor parenting, we now know this is untrue. Our best understanding is that autism results from some abnormality in brain development.

The term *autism* was first coined by Leo Kanner (1943) to describe a group of children who were distinctly different from children whose behaviors were classified under the label "childhood psychosis." Today the identification of autism is based on the developmental progress of the child and observations of the child's behavior. Autism is one of five disorders listed under Pervasive Developmental Disorders in the American Psychiatric Association's *Diagnostic and Statistical Manual* (1995). The other disorders include Rett's disorder, childhood disintegrative disorder, Apserger's disorder, and pervasive developmental disorder not otherwise specified. Autism shares a number of common characteristics with the other disorders listed, but the label includes a wide variety of conditions and behaviors.

In fact, variability is the underlying characteristic of children described as having autism (Tsai, 1998). This condition typically affects children's ability to communicate, to understand language, to play, and to relate to others. Some children may display behavior such as rocking or hand flapping. Others may resist changes in routine and may exhibit aggressive and/or self-injurious behaviors (such as head banging). These variations in children's behavior have led to myths about what it means to have autism ("Myths and Misunderstandings," 1985).

Myth: Children with autism never make eye contact. They do not look at you.
Fact: Many children do make eye contact and will look at you. Children who do not do this automatically may learn to develop eye contact with others over time.

Myth: Inside a child with autism is a genius.
Fact: Children with autism span the range of IQ scores from low to high. As is true of all children, their development can be very uneven. For example, one child may read perfectly but not be able to understand what is read. Another may have a talent for number facts but be challenged when faced with new situations typical of living in the community.

Myth: Children with autism do not speak.
Fact: Many children with autism are able to develop functional language. Others can develop communication skills using sign language, pictures, computers, or electronic devices.

Myth: Children with autism cannot show affection.
Fact: Many children with autism can and do give affection, but it often requires recipients to accept and give love on the child's terms. What those terms are may become evident only after numerous experiences governed by trial and error.

Early childhood professionals may encounter some children diagnosed as autistic by one physician and as having pervasive developmental disorder not otherwise specified (PDD-NOS) by another. This double labeling results from disagreement among professionals about the clear classification of these labels. What is important for you to know is that the recommended ways of addressing the children under these diagnostic categories are the same.

Hints for Success

In addition to the advice Andrew's mother provided to early childhood professionals in her narrative, here are some ways to support the development and learning of children with autism in your classroom (Dalrymple, 1992).

Situation 1: The child needs to learn to do a simple task such as getting dressed for outdoors or handwashing.
    What You Could Do to Be Helpful: Model what you want the child to do. Be consistent by repeating the same steps in the same order each time. Give children visual cues such as pictographs to help them remember what to do. Teach the skill in the actual place in which it will be used (such as handwashing at the bathroom sink). Then vary the settings (bathroom sink, outdoor faucet, kitchen sink) to help the child generalize the skill to new settings.

Situation 2: The child needs to learn to adapt to changes in routine.
    What You Could Do to Be Helpful: Use a visual cue such as a 5-minute warning sign before a new routine begins (e.g., clean-up time), as well as a verbal message that is delivered to the child personally. Provide the child with choices for replacement activities whenever possible (e.g., "After clean-up, you may swing on the swing or go down the slide"). Do not expect im-

mediate compliance. Give the child time to process and adjust his or her response. Physically support the child as necessary (e.g., lead the child gently toward a new activity; show the child how to begin cleaning up).

Situation 3: The child needs to learn to wait in appropriate situations.

What You Could Do to Be Helpful: Provide a timer that clicks off the minutes or an egg timer that visually moves water, oil, or sand to help the child follow the passage of time. Make sure routines and activities have beginnings and endings that are clear to the child. Teach children simple waiting strategies such as deep breathing or self-talk (e.g., "I can wait.").

Situation 4: The child jumps back or pulls away when touched.

What You Could Do to Be Helpful: Demonstrate some activities rather than physically assisting the child. Ask peers to help with demonstrations. Warn the child verbally that you will be touching him or her. Let the child get to know a person before asking the child to accept touch from that individual. Provide simple sensory activities such as sand and water play to gradually desensitize the child to tactile experiences.

Situation 5: The child holds his or her hands and arms over the ears or yells upon hearing certain sounds.

What You Could Do to Be Helpful: Provide appropriate ways for the child to avoid uncomfortable sounds, such as using earplugs or headsets or retreating to a quiet area. If you notice that certain sounds bother the child, provide information about the sound, when it will happen, and how to get away from it. Gradually desensitize the child to worrisome sounds through practice and by providing support and comfort when the sound occurs.

Situation 6: You want to help the child become more aware of how his or her actions affect others.

What You Could Do to Be Helpful: Provide clear, specific, positively stated rules about the situation (e.g., "Stand here" or "It is not okay to choke people"). Point out visual cues that will help the child interpret how the other person feels (e.g., "See her face. She is crying. She is sad."). Provide and practice simple scripts that teach appropriate social behaviors (e.g., "It's my turn next" or "I want it").

QUESTIONS FOR DISCUSSION

1. What are some things about Andrew that seemed typical for a child his age throughout this narrative?

2. If you were preparing to have Andrew in your preschool classroom, what would you do to prepare the other children for his arrival?
3. What lessons have you learned from Andrew's story?

RESOURCES FOR EDUCATORS AND PARENTS

Books

Janzen, J. (1999). *Autism: Facts and strategies for parents.* San Antonio, TX: Therapy Skill Builders.

Myles, B. S., & Southwick, J. (1999). *Asberger syndrome and difficult moments: Practical solutions for tantrums, rage and meltdowns.* Shawnee Mission, KS: Autism Asberger Publishing Company.

Quill, K. A. (1995). *Teaching children with autism: Strategies to enhance communication and socialization.* Albany, NY: Delmar.

Seroussi, K., & Rimland, B. (2000). *Unraveling the mystery of autism and pervasive develomental disorder: A mother's story of research and recovery.* New York: Simon & Schuster.

Simpson, R. L., & Zionts, P. (1999). *Autism: Information and resources for professionals and parents.* Austin, TX: Pro-Ed.

Organizations

The Autism National Committee
635 Ardmore Avenue
Ardmore, PA 19003
Membership information:
PO Box 6175
North Plymouth, MA 02362-6175
http://www.autcom.org (retrieved 5/15/01)
This organization, made up of families and professionals, provides useful information to both groups. Its mission is to promote inclusion of individuals with autism in the community and to offer practical strategies for positive behavioral support to those indivudals and their families.

The Autism Society of America
7910 Woodmont Avenue, Suite 300
Bethesda, MD 20814
Phone: (301) 657-0881
Fax: (301) 657-0869
This organization, which includes both laypersons and professionals, provides information and referral services to professionals and families. Local affiliates are available throughout the country.

Available Online

Autism/PDD Resources Network
http://www.autism-pdd.net/autism.htm
This Website provides access to a broad array of organizations and databases related to autism and the study of the brain. Sample topics include: diagnosis and testing, treatments, parent guide, special education services, related services, respite care, health insurance, state-by-state resources, and medical experts answer your questions online.

Center for the Study of Autism
http://ww.autism.org
The Center provides information about the research it conducts (in collaboration with the Autism Research Center in San Diego, California) and the efficacy of various interventions.

Online Asberger Syndrome Information and Support (O.A.S.I.S.)
http://www.udel.edu/bkrby/asberger (retrieved 5/14/01)
This site provides information on Asberger syndrome, including research and articles by individuals who have Asberger syndrome.

REFERENCES

American Psychiatric Association. (1995). *Diagnostic and Statistical Manual* (4th ed.). Washington, DC: Author.
Dalrymple, N. (1992). *Helpful responses to some of the behaviors of individuals with autism*. Bloomington, IN: Indiana Resource Center for Autism.
Kanner, L. (1943). Autistic disturbances of affective contact. *Nervous Child, 2,* 217–280.
Myths and misunderstandings. (1985, January). *The Advocate,* pp. 1–5.
Tsai, L. Y. (1998). *Pervasive developmental disorders* (Briefing Paper No. #FS20). Washington, DC: NICHCY.

C H A P T E R   3

Rosie

The Girl with the Million-Dollar Smile

The director of the Fairview Early Childhood Program thought, "This is the most physically challenged child we've ever been asked to enroll. I wonder if Dawn will be willing to work with her."

As she mounted the stairs to the classroom, the director mentally reviewed what she knew about 4-year-old Rosie Carmassi. Rosie had been born with cerebral palsy. According to her family, Rosie was a bright little girl who couldn't walk, couldn't talk, and couldn't voluntarily command any part of her body other than her eyes and her lips. A wheelchair user, hands partially closed in fists, Rosie was still in diapers. She was currently participating in a special education class with five other children who were severely impaired both physically and mentally. On the advice of their pediatrician, Rosie's parents were seeking a traditional preschool placement where Rosie could interact with typically developing children for half a day. However, that was easier said then done. They tried several early childhood programs in the community, only to find that none of them were comfortable taking on such a "needy" child. One program said they would do it if one of her parents participated in the classroom daily; another asked the parents to hire an aide to help their daughter at preschool; most simply said they had neither the staff nor the expertise to help.

Over a cup of tea, the director and the classroom teacher talked. After hearing everything the director had to say, Dawn replied, "I'd be interested in working with Rosie, but there's one thing I need to know. Can she smile?"

The teacher called Rosie's parents and found out she could smile and she could laugh. There were many things in life she enjoyed. Dawn said, "I'd love to be Rosie's teacher. I can't promise I'll know exactly what to do, but I'll try. When can she come for a visit?" Thus began Rosie's involvement in the Fairview program.

HER TEACHER TELLS ROSIE'S STORY

Preparing for Rosie's Arrival

Meeting Rosie and Her Family

The director told me that when she called the family to invite them to observe a typical morning, Rosie's dad began to cry. They had been turned down by so many other programs, he couldn't believe we would actually enroll her. Her parents came by themselves and just watched for an hour or so during a time when children were there. Later, they brought Rosie to see her new school with no children present. She came into the classroom and saw the toys and met me. [*She was in a portable stroller.*] It was my first chance to talk with her. I told her about a typical day and some of the things she would do at school.

I remember when they left I felt overwhelmed. I had worked with some other children with cerebral palsy before, but I had never worked with a child as severely challenged as she was. The things I learned with the other children didn't seem to help me much. At first, all I could think about was that I didn't know enough about cerebral palsy. But, when I thought about it more, I reasoned that you need to know the child you are working with, not just the condition. So, my first job was getting to know her and learning what her parents wanted or what they expected of us.

Clarifying Goals

Rosie was to come into my classroom of 4-year-olds in the fall of the year. Before each year begins, we do home visits with all of our children and their families. So I did my first home visit with Rosie and her family. As part of my home visit, we talked about her parents' goals for Rosie in the program. I admit I was worried about Rosie's special education needs because I don't have the training to do occupational therapy or anything like that. Rosie's parents made it clear that their primary goal was for her to be around other children. They weren't even that concerned that she actually interact with them; they just wanted her to be around typically developing children so she could see, hear, and experience being in their vicinity. She had no children her age in the neighborhood, and none of the children in her special education class was of normal intelligence. The pediatrician told them Rosie was bright and needed the stimulation that typically developing children could offer. I figured we could provide that.

Briefing Children and Families

Rosie's parents gave me a couple of cute photographs of her. She was in a clown suit for Halloween in one of them; she was laughing in her wheelchair in the other. In each picture, she looked very appealing and sweet. She had a wide grin—a real million-dollar smile. I wouldn't have said "no" to having Rosie in my room if she couldn't smile, but knowing she could made things a whole lot easier. I had a starting point for working with her and with the other children and families in our program.

Initially, I was worried that kids would be frightened or somehow put off by the chair and Rosie's lack of body control. I also learned that she made a variety of sounds that could be startling if you weren't expecting them. So, it was important to me to prepare children and parents before open-house day.

I took the photographs of Rosie on all the home visits for the class. As part of my home visit routine that year, I explained to the children that we were going to have a really extra-special little person in our classroom who was going to need lots of help from all of us because there were lots of things that she couldn't do yet, as well as things she couldn't do at all. But, I said, she likes to play and to have fun, and she really wants to have friends. So, we are all going to help her do those things this year.

The children also had a chance to ask questions in advance, like "Why is she in that chair?" and "How will she play with me?" I answered as best I could. Sometimes, I said we'd have to ask Rosie or we'd have to discover the answer together. Most children seemed to look forward to meeting her, and everyone knew her name.

I also talked to each child's parent(s). I told them that they could always call me or the director for clarification with any questions anytime during the schoolyear. I don't recall that anyone did, but later families said they appreciated knowing they could talk to someone at school if they needed to.

I think this advanced preparation really set up the parents as much as it did the children. The families that year were very supportive in the way they talked to their children at the end of each day about things that happened at school, including things that happened with Rosie.

At the first parent meeting of the year, Rosie was not the main focus of attention, but somehow her name came up. Parents were genuinely interested in her progress. I remember her mom was there, and the other parents who had been in to observe or work in the classroom told her several positive things about her daughter. She, in turn, told them some things Rosie had communicated about the classroom and their children. It was a friendly, informative time for everyone.

Structuring the Physical Environment

Before the first day of school, I did a lot of basic things for Rosie that I do for every child. I made her a name tag, I put her photograph in her cubby, I made sure we had some materials her parents said she enjoyed at home, such as music and some familiar storybooks. One other thing I did was check out the space for the wheelchair. It was motorized and very bulky. I invited Rosie and her family to visit the building a few days before the open house. They brought her chair, and we saw places that were a tight squeeze. I had to do some rearranging of tables and pathways so we could maneuver it around the classroom more easily.

A Typical Day for Rosie

We follow a traditional preschool routine, 3 hours a day, 4 days a week. Our schedule includes outdoor time, small-group activities (children rotate between designated areas), and circle time. We also have what some people would call free choice. This is a time during which children move about the room and self-select various learning centers in which to play—blocks, art, games, puzzles, pretend play, science, math manipulatives, books, computer, woodworking, snack, and a pet center. We tried to incorporate Rosie into the classroom so she would have contact with other children. She participated in each part of the day as fully as possible. I am the head teacher, and I usually have two or three college students who help out each day. So part of my responsibility is to teach the 19 preschoolers in the class and part involves guiding the college students.

Rosie came to us in the mornings and went to her special education classroom in the afternoons [see Figure 3.1 for the morning schedule]. Her father dropped her off at Fairview, then a school bus picked her up at the end of the session. She had lunch and an afternoon program of activities at her other school. She got all kinds of therapy at the special education program. I know she got physical therapy every day, and she

Figure 3.1. Rosie's morning.

ROSIE'S MORNING

8:25–8:40	*Arrival of children*: children greeted at cars by head teachers/student teachers; escorted to playground by other students; attendance is taken and children choose play areas
8:30–9:00	*Outdoor play*: children engage in planned and spontaneous activities; adults supervise and join in as appropriate
9:00	*Outdoor clean-up*: materials put away
9:05	*Transition to classroom*: children are escorted to room in a group with adult support
9:15–9:35	*Small-group activities*: children participate in teacher-planned activities in small group; adults supervise as assigned
9:40–10:00	*Large group*: adults support children in participating and listening to stories, songs, discussions, and so on
10:00–11:00	*Learning centers*: children select areas of interest; adults supervise as appropriate
11:00–11:10	*Clean-up*: children and adults work together to put materials away, scrub tables, and so on
11:10–11:20	*Evaluation time*: children and adults return to small group areas to complete evaluation of day
11:20–11:30	*Prepare for dismissal and transition group*: children gather belongings; adults assist as needed
11:30	*Transition to dismissal area*: group moves to dismissal area; adults support safety on stairs
11:35–11:45	*Dismissal of children*: head teacher and student teachers load children into cars; other students support as assigned

---

was also learning to work with a voice computer. Most of her afternoons were spent one-on-one with a teacher or therapist. She had little contact with the afternoon children.

Connections Among Settings

I saw Rosie's dad frequently because he was the one who brought her each morning. We would chat a little at drop-off time most days. We didn't sit down or talk formally—our interactions were brief. However, over time they really added up, and we both felt like we passed a lot of information back and forth—just little things like what had gone on at home or in her other program or what we had done at Fairview the previous day.

I met with the special education staff a couple of times during the year. I visited their classroom and saw what it was like. They also came and observed her in our program.

We had a notebook that we sent back and forth—it was a three-way kind of thing between home, school, and the special education setting [see Figure 3.2]. I've done this with other children with special needs, and it is helpful. We would share a little something about her day—so we all knew things that were going on and we could talk to her about those things. It enabled us to let her know we were all interconnected. I think that was important.

Communicating with Rosie

Rosie could make some very limited sounds but didn't have enough control that you could use those for much regular communication. She really depended on her eyes. She could roll her eyes upward for "yes" and downward for "no." She could also move them to the left and right to signal direction and look at something to make her needs known.

Rosie had a picture board that we used sometimes, and that was really great. It was a circular piece of cardboard with pictures displayed in wedges, kind of like a pie. She had a few pictures of typical things she might need or want in the classroom, such as water or the toilet, and some pictures for areas in the room, such as puzzles or pretend play [see Figure 3.3]. The board was always available, and she would look at a part of it to indicate what she wanted. Then we could discuss with her where she wanted to spend her time and things like that.

We had some frustrating times early in the year, Rosie and I, because when she would want something and I would not know what it

Figure 3.2 An example of preschool notebook entries by Rosie's teacher, her pre-primary special education teacher, and her mother.

1/8/98	Rosie had a wonderful Christmas vacation. We spent the last week in Miami—temps 80–84 degrees, sunny, swimming every day. She is not eager to be back, I'm afraid. We tried to tell her that kids who live in Florida have to go to school and don't get to swim all day and go out every night to dinner with Grandma and Grandpa. She's not convinced.

—Mrs. G. [Mom]

1/8/98	Hi. Welcome back. Rosie is "stacking" in her wheelchair—is there a change in seating? Just curious. She ate a good lunch.

—Audrey [special education teacher]

1/8/98	I hate to be out of it—please define "stacking." Rosie spent today at a tea party with Michelle and Kelly and Laura. They discussed vacations, served "milkshakes" and muffins. Ryan asked Rosie several times to come and see his block structure. She finally agreed.

—Dawn [early childhood teacher]

1/9/98	Dawn, "stacking" is a postural problem where the head is tilted back and her shoulders flop forward. Rosie will sit up if we say, "Can you pick your shoulder up better?" or anything similar, and she is very proud that she is able to do so.

—Audrey

1/12/98	Rosie is bringing dinosaur stickers for sharing—the other kids can have one to take home.

—Mrs. G.

1/12/98	Stickers were a hit! Rosie would like to also share with her Adams School friends. Rosie enjoyed reaching for and grasping scarves in the gym. She chose pink ones (we didn't have purple). She elected to "supervise" the art area where Michelle and Kyle asked her for choices for the Boxosaurus decorations.

—Dawn

1/13/98	Rosie was very rigid in PT today. She relaxed during "rolling inside the barrel"—her favorite activity—but tightened up when she attempted any play activities or position changes. I asked her is she was upset, "no"; unhappy— "no." So I'm not sure what the problem was.

—Audrey

1/14/98	Rosie was able to say "yes" or "no" (with her eyes) to answer, "Mother, may I?" She seemed to like this. We measured things in the room, including her chair, with cubes at small group.

—Dawn

Figure 3.3. Rosie's communication board.

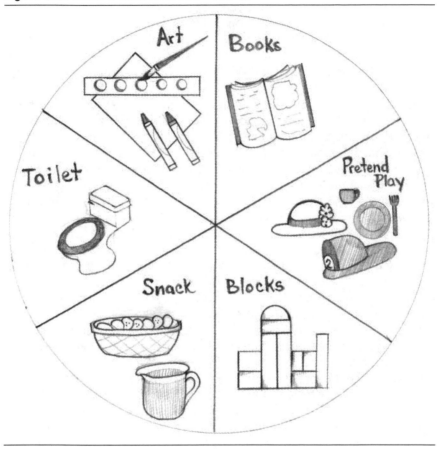

was, she would get really frustrated and cry. Sometimes when this happened, she would get so upset she would have a tantrum—crying hard and making a kind of howling sound. Her face would become contorted, and she would drool profusely (this was frightening to the other children). At first, I felt so bad I'd try everything to give her what she wanted. Then I thought, this isn't helping her. We've got to help her stop and get back in control so she can cope and we can figure out a way to communicate. That's when I started using time-out. I felt just awful when I had to do that. But she would get so out of control, I had to get her out of the classroom so she could calm down. When these incidents came up, I would say, "You are out of control right now. We are going out into the hall until you are in control. Then you can come back into the classroom." Those were the words I used each time.

Getting her out of the situation that upset her and giving her a chance to calm down without an audience helped. Rosie didn't want to be away from the classroom—she really wanted to be in there. These incidents eventually happened less and less. The first time I did a time-out, it was very upsetting to me; I felt so mean. Here was this physically helpless little person, and I was taking her out of the classroom and telling her to get in control. I admired her courage and didn't know how she put up with all she had to put up with (her limitations and our inability to understand what she was trying to get across).

Getting beyond the tantrums was a major milestone. That happened once Rosie came to trust me and understood that I was trying to figure out whatever she was wanting—I was not deliberately thwarting her in the world. I am sure that sometimes it must have seemed like I was being insensitive to her, because it was obvious that she wanted something and I was just not doing it. She also became better able to handle frustration and try an alternate strategy when her first attempts at communication didn't work.

Sometime around January, Rosie's parents told us she was getting a voice computer. They were very excited about it. When it arrived, they brought it in to show everyone how it worked. It had a grid with words similar to her picture board that could be activated by a stylus Rosie held in her fist. Her special education setting was planning on using it extensively. We tried it for several weeks. However, we began to realize that the machine was interfering with Rosie's interactions with the other children. It was cumbersome, and she had little motor control as of yet, so getting it to work was agonizingly slow. It got in the way of the faster-paced communication with her eyes that Rosie had previously enjoyed. We talked with her parents and the special education staff, and everyone agreed that we should go back to our other ways of communicating. They would keep on working with the machine in the afternoons and at home. I was so relieved. I thought they would all be so disappointed, but it was really getting in the way of what was going on in our classroom. It was a distraction rather than a help at that point.

Playing in the Classroom

Something I was really surprised and pleased about happened early in the year. In my classroom, I divide the children into small groups of about five children each for a short portion of the day. These groups stay together throughout the year. Each group has an opportunity to think of a name for themselves. This consists of children making suggestions, talking about the choices, and picking one of their ideas. I was amazed to discover that Rosie was the one who thought up the name for her group. She really did and they all decided to use her name! By using her eyes and with the help of a perceptive adult, she looked at a picture in the room and indicated that it was her choice—red balloons. All the children thought that was really cool, so Red Balloons became their name for the year. Rosie had named them, and it was only the second week of school. After that, I thought that if she could be the one who made the choice in this group and could communicate, then we would be fine. And we were.

One of the activities Rosie really liked was body tracing. We got her out of her chair, and one of the kids traced her. Then we got her back into her chair, and a couple of little girls decorated the tracing. Rosie directed the whole thing by moving her eyes either "yes" or "no" to the colors they were choosing. That was an interesting experience. She took home the body tracing she had directed.

Rosie liked pretend play an awful lot. The children would involve her by putting things in her hands, fixing tea, and giving her the baby to hold.

I remember her playing games at the magnet board. The children would spend a lot of time working with her, matching letters and pictures, spelling some simple words they all knew. In each case she would communicate with her eyes whether they were doing it right or not—that was exciting for everybody. We [staff and children] got to be pretty good at asking the right kinds of questions that she could answer with her eyes.

Making Friends

During the first few weeks of school, the special education teachers mentioned that they were trying to help Rosie learn how to handle a spoon. To support their efforts, we decided to work on similar hand skills, like holding a paintbrush. Every day one of the teachers worked with Rosie at the easel, having her grip a brush in her hand and attempt to make strokes on the paper. One day our director came in and watched for a while. Later, she said she noticed that we were taking a long time for these sessions and that Rosie was spending a major portion of every free-choice period isolated at the easel. She wondered if that was the best use of her time in our program. I thought about it and realized that we had lost sight of Rosie's prime reason for being in the classroom—to have contact with the children. We changed our approach and concentrated instead on goals that couldn't be addressed in the other setting, such as playing with children her age.

The first thing I did was give each child a chance to be Rosie's buddy for the day. That child would make sure she knew what was available in the classroom and that she got around to some of the activities. This gave each child a chance to interact with her one-on-one.

We have a job chart in our classroom that is part of the daily routine. Each day a few children have a chance to do something important in the classroom, like water the plants or act as the line leader going downstairs. One of the jobs during Rosie's year in the group was for someone to accompany her up and down on the elevator when we went outdoors or when it was time to go home. Little things like that made her more appealing to the children—they vied for the chance to do that job.

Rosie was in a motorized wheelchair, which was a massive thing to deal with. Getting her in and out was really hard. So we didn't get her out much at first. Suddenly I realized that this was not good. She was too separated from the other children—the chair was huge and she was not physically approachable. So we took her out of the chair on the playground, and somebody would slide down the slide with her or she would be on the tire swing with the kids with somebody holding her there. We got to where we took her out of the chair every day at group time so she could sit down on the floor and be with the children instead of being so removed from them. She needed to be physically supported during those times because she couldn't support herself in a sitting position. I had her sit on the lap of an adult or tucked into the adult's side, and it worked out very well.

Over the year Rosie made friends. All the children were good to her, but she had particular friends who sought her out and really spent a lot of time with her. They were very supportive, but they weren't just doing it to be prosocial; they enjoyed their interactions with her.

One of the boys enjoyed teasing her—not in an unkind way, but in the way that children do when they are having fun with one another. For instance, Rosie couldn't do puzzles physically, but she would direct the other children in doing the puzzles by looking at the pieces and using her eyes to signal where they went. I don't know exactly how it worked, but it did. One little boy would do what she wanted for a while, then he would grin and he would do something wrong. She would laugh, and he would laugh. He would deliberately go against what she had told him to do. He would pretend that he didn't get it, and it became a funny thing. When that happened, I thought, "Boy, something great is happening here!" I know he was teasing her, but it was all in good fun. She enjoyed it very much and laughed really hard each time it happened. It was clear that they both enjoyed these moments.

School picture day definitely demonstrated how much the children enjoyed Rosie. In our school, we take group pictures of each class. When it was our turn, many children wanted to have Rosie be next to them for the photo. The photographer ended up taking three different pictures so a variety of children could be clustered around her chair. Her parents enjoyed hearing how popular she was.

Answering Children's Questions

Children were curious about Rosie. Some wondered what had happened to her to make her the way she was. I told them that she was born with something that interfered with the way that she could move. So she couldn't talk and she couldn't walk the way we could. I explained to them that it was often frustrating for her not to be able to do these things. Even though I talked openly about the fact that many things about Rosie were different, I also stressed that she was like them in many ways. Her favorite color was purple, and she really liked fairy tales, puppets, and music. Hearing that Rosie liked things that they liked helped the children be more open and accepting of her rather than seeing her as this strange creature all propped up in a wheelchair.

The children wanted to know a lot of things about Rosie's wheelchair. Her father came in for a group time early in the year and showed everyone how it worked. The class thought that was pretty great stuff.

Challenges in the Classroom

At first, when Rosie got upset about things, all the adults would try to cater to her and give her anything she wanted. Everyone just felt so sorry for this little girl in the wheelchair who couldn't talk or move about freely. As a result, she was getting rewarded for some very inappropriate behavior, and it kept getting worse. I sat the adult assistants down and said, "We are not helping Rosie when we give in to her every whim." I asked them if they would say "yes" to some of the things she wanted if other children asked for them (such as not washing her hands before snack or not waiting her turn on the slide). Everyone agreed they wouldn't. Then I said, "We are here to help her. The way we are going to help her is to not let her behave like that." We all worked hard on this.

I tried to be very matter-of-fact with Rosie when we tackled something hard, like handling a crayon. I didn't make a big deal of it—I was encouraging but not too effusive. I wanted her to get the idea that eventually she would be successful and that I just naturally believed that would be the case. I think it helped her to keep trying. Some days I would go home and cry because it was so hard to watch her struggle, but I was matter-of-fact in her presence.

Changing Rosie's diaper was a challenge. She was a tall child, and getting her out of her chair was a big job in itself. There were so many straps and braces. I would take her out of the classroom and put her on the floor on a pad (there was no way I could lift her onto a table). She liked these times and often moved about, just to tease me. She usually didn't do that until she was cleaned up, which was good.

Lasting Effects

I came to see Rosie as a strong little girl—not physically strong, but very strong in will, very determined. She tried very hard. I think this will stand her in good stead later in life. She is definitely bright. Her many strengths include having a good sense of humor, not getting thrown or upset by things the children could do that she couldn't to the point that she wouldn't try, and finding ways to connect with other people. Rosie was very much inspired by the other children and enjoyed being with them. She really engaged in the "kid" culture of the classroom.

We had a wonderful year! The children made it a success as much as the staff and I did. I said afterwards, "I don't know if this year I just happened to have the most wonderful group of thoughtful, gentle, kind, and considerate children or if having the opportunity to interact with Rosie helped them to be kind, gentle, thoughtful, and considerate." They weren't just kind with her; they were very prosocial in general. They were a great group of kids. I think she impacted them a lot.

I would say this to anyone contemplating working with a child like Rosie: "Get to know her and the family as much as you can. Put that first, before you focus on the special needs the child may have." I worked hard, but I really enjoyed it. It was a wonderful experience for me and for the college students in the classroom. It was a terrific experience for my kids. That's my advice: "Enjoy it!"

Epilogue

Rosie is now in the second grade. She spends the first half of her day in a traditional classroom and her afternoons in a special education setting. Rosie is reading. She communicates using a light-sensitive Liberator, a form of assisted technology. The Liberator is a rectangular box, similar in size to a laptop computer. It sits at Rosie's eye level and attaches to her motorized wheelchair. The surface facing Rosie is divided into squares programmed with messages that she often uses. A symbol in each grid helps her remember the word or phrase it contains. It is also possible for Rosie to spell out things using a regular keyboard. Rosie activates the appropriate square or key using a light sensor she wears on a headband. When she activates the machine, it speaks mechanically in a female voice. It works much like the picture board she had in her preschool classroom. Her family reports that the Liberator has truly liberated Rosie, making it much easier for her to communicate with others.

Another addition to Rosie's life is her helping dog, Penny. Penny is a golden retriever who has been specially trained to assist people with physical challenges to do simple tasks like open a door, turn off a light, or carry things. Rosie loves Penny, and Penny loves her. They make a great team. Rosie's parents note that Penny makes it easier for people to approach Rosie and that she has eased Rosie's transition into elementary school by making her more independent.

INFORMATION FOR EDUCATORS ABOUT CEREBRAL PALSY

Rosie was born with a medical condition known as cerebral palsy (CP), which affects control of the muscles in the body. "Cerebral" refers to the brain, and "palsy" refers to the person's inability to use muscles in a typical way. It is estimated that nearly 500,000 children and adults in the United States manifest one or more symptoms of cerebral palsy. These individuals are affected to different degrees, from minimal impairment that is barely discernible to such severe impairment that the child has little control of his or her body. Currently 5,000 babies a year are diagnosed with the condition. In addition, 1,200 to 1,500 preschool-age children are annually recognized to have CP.

CP is caused by injury to the developing brain before, during, or after birth. Complications in the birth process may lead to an insufficient amount of oxygen reaching the brain, causing brain lesions that result in CP. Other causes may be infection of the mother with certain viruses in early pregnancy. Because the condition is not inherited, it is referred to as congenital cerebral palsy. (A less common type of cerebral palsy—acquired CP—may result from a head injury, usually occurring before age 2.) CP is not an illness or disease, and it is certainly not contagious. It doesn't get worse, but it is not something people "grow out of." Children who have CP will have it all their lives.

Characteristics of the most common type of CP (spastic cerebral palsy) may be stiff, jerky movements, difficulty moving from one position to another, and difficulty letting go of an object in the hand. Children who have

CP in both their arms and legs often have trouble moving the muscles in their face and throat, making it difficult for them to talk and eat.

Professionals frequently classify the type of physical impairment people have by referring to the part of the body that is affected. These terms are grouped together in what is called a topographical classification system.

Monoplegia: one limb
Paraplegia: legs only
Hemiplegia: one-half of the body
Triplegia: three limbs—usually one arm and both legs
Quadriplegia: all four limbs
Diplegia: most affected in the legs rather than the arms
Double hemiplegia: most affected in the arms rather than the legs

The specific location of the movement impairment is correlated with the location of the brain damage that has occurred (Turnbull, Turnbull, Shank, & Leal, 1999).

Through training and therapy, people with CP can improve their functioning. Management of CP includes early identification and support for movement, learning, speech, hearing, and social and emotional development. Medications, surgery, and physical aids are often found to be useful to improve muscle coordination. Some special tools that are helpful for many children with CP are: wheelchair, walker, helmet, adapted silverware and pencils, a prone board that supports a child in a standing position, and communication aids such as picture posters, alphabet boards, or computers (Children's Medical Center, 2001).

HINTS FOR SUCCESS

In addition to the teaching strategies Dawn talked about in her interview, here are some other ways to work more effectively with children who have CP.

1. Make sure children are adequately strapped/propped in any chair in which they are functioning. Because children with CP spend a lot of time sitting, it is important that they sit in the most appropriate position possible. Use physical supports to help children sit upright, such as bolsters, wedges, or beanbags. These are pillowlike objects that allow comfortable positioning and can be adapted to the individual child.
2. If you hold a child with cerebral palsy on your lap, have the child's legs straddle one of yours and hold the child around the middle. If the

child sits on the floor, have him or her sit with the legs in front and together, either bent at the knee or straight out. Do not have the child sit pretzel-style, as is common in many preschool classrooms (Deiner, 1993).

3. Allow children enough time to ask questions or make comments. Many children with CP have difficulty communicating verbally. If they have speech, they may speak slowly and be hard to understand. If they use a communication aid, it will take time for them to construct their message. Be patient—it may take more time than you're used to waiting. Tell yourself to listen quietly rather than feeling like you have to talk to fill the gaps of silence. Just as you do with all children, communicate at eye level. Pay attention to children's voice tone and facial expressions as well as their words. Allow children enough time to finish—don't interrupt or complete children's sentences for them. If you don't understand a child's message, honestly explain your failure to understand and ask the child to try again. Be alert for frustration in a child and acknowledge such feelings as they arise. When children with CP are with other people, talk directly to them. Avoid talking to a child through others or talking about the child as though he or she were not there (Miller & Bachrach, 1998; Turnball, et al., 1999).

4. Look for each child's strengths rather than focusing on what the child cannot do. Through experience, you will learn what the child with CP can do for him- or herself and what assistance the child will need.

5. Listen to the parents of the child and follow their lead—they know their child best and have a good idea of what to expect from their son or daughter. Parents usually want their child with CP to be treated, whenever possible, in the same way as any other child. Inclusion is the key word.

6. Provide information about the individual child to assistants and classroom volunteers. Many adults who have not spent time with a child with CP are apprehensive about it at first. Point out the child's strengths, interests, and abilities. Encourage concerned adults to ask questions and to read about cerebral palsy.

QUESTIONS FOR DISCUSSION

1. What are some of the ways Dawn helped Rosie and the other children get the most from this experience?
2. How did the teacher and director make the family an active partner in Rosie's preschool education?
3. What lessons did you learn from Rosie's story?

RESOURCES FOR EDUCATORS AND PARENTS

Books

Cogher, L., Savage, E., & Smith, M. (1992). *Cerebral palsy: The child and young person*. Philadelphia: Lippincott-Raven.
Miller, F., & Bachrach, S. (1998). *Cerebral palsy: A complete guide for caregiving*. Baltimore: Johns Hopkins University Press.

Available Online

Alfred I. Dupont Institute, Wilmington, Delaware
gait.aidi.udel.edu/res695/homepage/pd_ortho/clinics/c_palsy/cpweb.htm

Cerebral Palsy Support Network
www.home.aone.net.au/cpsn/
This voluntary network based in Melbourne, Australia, provides support, advice, and assistance to parents.

Children's Medical Center, University of Virginia
www.med.Virginia.edu/cmc/tutorials/cp

Parent Support for Kids with CP
www.geocities.com/heartland/bluffs/6928/index.html

REFERENCES

Children's Medical Center of the University of Virginia. (2001). Tutorials for Families, Cerebral Palsy.
http://www.med.virginia.edu/cmc/cmchome.html [click on tutorials] (retrieved 5/15/01)
Deiner, P. L. (1993). *Resources for teaching children with diverse abilities*. New York: Harcourt Brace Jovanovich.
Miller, F., & Bachrach, S. (1998). *Cerebral palsy: A complete guide for caregiving*. Baltimore: Johns Hopkins University Press.
Turnbull, A., Turnbull, R., Shank, M., & Leal, D. (1999). *Exceptional lives: Special education in today's schools*. Upper Saddle River, NJ: Merrill.

CHAPTER 4

Sara

"A Person's a Person, No Matter How Small"

Sara's mom knew there was something very different about her even before she was born. "When I was almost 5 months pregnant Sara quit growing in me." Sitting in her small midwestern kitchen, Sara's mom describes the early signs she experienced and the diagnosis that made her cry.

Editor's note: the subtitle for this chapter, "A Person's a Person, No Matter How Small," is taken from *Horton Hears a Who* (Dr. Seuss, 1954).

SARA'S MOTHER BEGINS THE STORY

My doctor sent me right away to a hospital that had heart specialists; I had to go there every 3 weeks. He thought he had detected a mass in the baby's heart and was concerned it could result in congestive heart failure. The doctors did ultrasound and measured every bone in her body. They came to the conclusion that the baby had a condition known as dwarfism [*a genetic condition resulting in smaller stature; there are over 100 diagnosed types of dwarfism* (Little People of America, 2000)]. They weren't sure, but that was the best they could come up with. The heart specialist said he didn't feel that congestive heart failure was going to be an issue, but I remember another doctor telling me, "You'll see I'm not wrong, it's dwarfism." That was real hard to deal with emotionally. Months later, after worrying and wondering about that, I went back for more tests, and they said they were wrong. It wasn't dwarfism after all; the baby had started growing again, but at a very slow rate.

With more tests, the doctors recognized some unusual things: The baby's legs were quite short, and her head was bigger than they expected. When the time came, she was born by cesarean section. They checked her all over and did a cardiogram on her. They said her heart was fine, but something was not right.

When Sara was a year old, she looked like she was about 8 months. I mean she was real little, and the doctor kept saying "You know, this can't be right," but he didn't say what it was. As she neared her third birthday, it had been a year and a half since she had grown at all; she was extremely small. So they started doing physical examinations every 3 months to see whether she was growing even a little; she wasn't. We'd run into friends, and they'd say, "Oh, my God, she is little." They would have a child a year or 2 younger who was quite a bit bigger than Sara. It made me wonder, but since I'm short, we didn't think it was something to worry about.

Diagnosis

In kindergarten, when Sara had just turned 5, she was so incredibly small compared to the other kids that the doctor sent us to the nearby university medical school to see an endocrinologist [*a doctor specializing in growth and hormone problems*]. Dr. Cradit recognized what to look for right away. He looked at her neck and feet, and he did a blood test, which came back positive. She had Turner syndrome. That's when I started reading all I could about this condition and learned that growing is really a big thing.

The doctor pointed out some other signs of Turner syndrome—her hairline, which grows low on the neck. He also asked Sara to make a fist, and he pointed out that she didn't have the end knuckle. I mean there was a knuckle, but it didn't show. Webbing is also a sign—Sara has it on the neck, but hers is very minimal. [Neck webbing means she has connecting tissue between the shoulder and partway up the sides of the neck.] Some children with Turner's have webbed feet, too, but Sara doesn't. Girls with Turner syndrome have a lot of health problems later in life. A lot have high blood pressure and diabetes.

The hardest thing to accept is that Sara can't have kids. Girls with Turner's don't have menstrual cycles and don't develop breasts. Learning that was devastating . . . but hopefully there will be research that someday will be able to do something. Sara doesn't know that. She's not ready for that information yet.

Some girls with Turner's also have learning difficulties. Not all of them—but because I was so worried, I thought she was going to have every one of them. [Sara's parents and teachers are gradually becoming aware of her learning problems.]

Treatment Begins

In December, when Sara was 5, they started giving her injections of growth hormones. That was her worst nightmare. She had to have one shot every night before bedtime, and she was always scared. I learned how to give them, then later her stepdad learned. For the first 7 months, it was really terrible. Sara would tell us she didn't like us. She'd scream and kick her legs around. We had to restrain her by holding her arms and legs to give her a shot.

Doctors tell us Sara will have to have shots until she's 14 years old. In the beginning, getting shots affected everything she did and thought about. She was constantly asking, "Do I have to have my shot? Do I have to have it now? How much longer?" At one point, she stopped eating because of it—she was so worried we were going to give a shot to her. In the morning she'd ask, "Do I have to have it tonight?" She went to school with that on her mind every day. It was so hard on her.

When she went to her dad's, I felt very uncomfortable letting her go, because he would have to give the shots. I wanted to be the one giving the shots and the one to hold her. When she was there, she'd be sobbing and he'd say, "You're not going to cry in my house. You don't need to cry." She would have to put up a strong front. But you know, I think she needed to cry.

It's a big day once a month when she gets measured at my father's house. Sara likes to be measured, because it shows she's growing, even if it's just a little. The shots are helping, but she's still real small. Her neighborhood friend is a whole year younger, and she's about 4 inches taller.

Sara at School

Sara didn't like her first year of kindergarten very much. Her preschool teachers had said maybe she shouldn't go to kindergarten because she was so small and her birthday is in October. But after thinking it over, we decided to send her anyway that fall.

One thing I noticed was that the other kids, and also some of the adults in the school, treated her as small. They thought she was so cute, and they would do things for her instead of encouraging her to try them herself. The children would fight about who was going to be her partner. Everybody thought she was a baby. As a result, she acted really immature. I mean, she showed some definite problems with learning compared to the others; she had a real rough start. [*See Figure 4.1 for a graphic representation of milestones in Sara's life.*]

I don't know if it was overwhelming for her, but she was way behind in school. She was a bit younger, and some kids could do their numbers and knew how to write their name; Sara didn't. All the other kids were up to speed, and Sara was lagging behind. She also was sick a lot; she had asthma and pneumonia that year. A lung collapsed, and she missed a great deal of school. It was a really hard year for her.

After we got the diagnosis of Turner syndrome, I told Sara's kindergarten teacher, "What I know is that she is going to get some shots." After that conversation, sometimes her teacher would ask, "How's it going?" I'd say, "Things are not going too well. Sara is not eating well, and she's not very focused on anything but the shots." She slept, ate, and got shots; that's all there was for her.

At the mid-year parent conference, her kindergarten teacher told me that Sara's progress wasn't what they expected, and she was not likely to advance. I realized then that she wasn't looking at first grade for the next year. They said she wasn't staying on track, and she wasn't sitting still. The teacher recommended her for a special program where an aide took kids out in small groups twice a week to play learning games. It was supposed to help kids catch up.

One time, they had their early learning consultant come look at her for the morning. After that, the teacher didn't meet with me, but instead

Figure 4.1. Sara's time line.

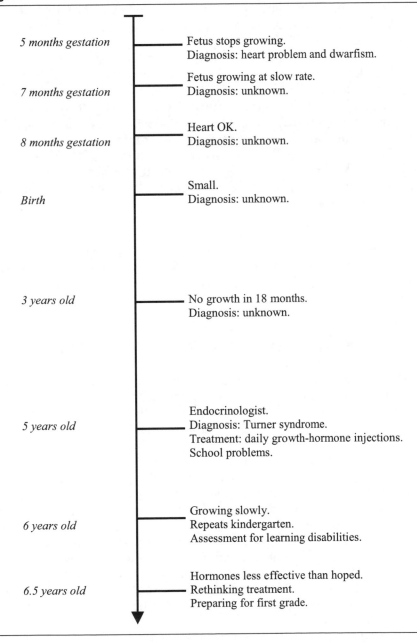

I met with the consultant. She told me some things about Sara's school behavior—her sociability and problem solving. She was very detailed about how Sara was doing in the classroom. She said Sara wasn't writing, but she drew pictures.

I continued to feel very uncomfortable about her kindergarten. I felt that the teacher was out of patience with Sara. Sometimes she said she didn't like her teacher. Sometimes I would ask the teacher, when I picked Sara up at school, "How is she doing?" and "Is she getting any better?" The teacher would say, "Oh, fine," or she would say, "She doesn't listen," right in front of Sara. At times the classroom aide would say, "No, I think it's worsening," but not give me much detail. Then Sara would always come home and say that she had to sit in time-out again. I felt they were putting her in time-out without explaining why. I felt she was always in time-out.

———————

Sara repeated kindergarten in a different school in an all-day, every-day program. After our interview with Sara's mother, we visited her current kindergarten teacher, Allen Bayshore. It was just as the schoolyear was ending.

HER TEACHER TELLS ABOUT SARA'S PROGRESS

I'd love to tell you about Sara. She is growing more but is still the smallest in the class. Unfortunately, at the end of the spring quarter I heard from her mother that the daily hormone shots were losing their effect, and that really worried us both. We're not sure what's going to happen with that.

In the fall I attended a "staffing," a meeting with the principal, Sara's mother, a social worker, the school psychologist, and others to discuss Sara's problems and possible intervention strategies. Our district uses meetings like this to determine and evaluate supports that will be tried before the child is recommended for special education services. As a follow-up to that meeting, I started using a variety of visual cues in the classroom, such as a new colorful schedule board, to point out what happens next and attempt to keep Sara focused. The strategy worked wonderfully with all the other kids; they loved it. However, Sara never noticed it, even when others pointed it out to her. She was unable to use that information.

Sara is highly distracted by sounds, and while she could often focus on a social issue like a problem with a friend, she could not attend to what I wanted her to do, like listening to a story. Sara would come to book club, the name for our weekly small-group activity focused on literacy, but within a minute she'd be looking around. She was somewhat interested in books, but she couldn't attend to them for long and was constantly distracted.

She had a really hard time with rhyme and demonstrated no phonological awareness [*the ability to recognize and manipulate sounds in words, highly correlated with children's success in beginning reading. Awareness develops in stages: becoming aware that language is made of words, that words are made of parts (syllables), and that syllables are made of sounds (phonemes).*].

Sara remained the best artist in the class. She enjoyed making constructions in the art center, and her penmanship was developing. So I would say she did fairly well in fine-motor tasks.

I learned a lot about Sara this year, but she remains a bit of a mystery to me. Here it is the end of her second year in kindergarten, and she can only recognize 24 out of 52 letters, mostly uppercase. On the other hand, she can match symbols, but her ability to do patterning is very poor. She has no recognition of and cannot extend patterns. We decided she should go on to first grade in the fall. They are planning to test her for learning disabilities and to provide reading interventions for her. She would not get what she needs by staying in this building. That building has a resource room for children in special education.

Perhaps the best thing is the fact that her first-grade teacher will be looping with the class [*going on to second grade with them at the end of the year*]. That will probably help Sara and her family, too. I hope that being a struggling reader and writer doesn't negatively affect her self-esteem. My hope for Sara is that she reaches her physical potential and someday becomes an artist, something she's good at. This is a note I wrote on the bottom of her report card: "Sara is a sweet, bright child. As much as she could be a challenge, she made me a better teacher by keeping me on my toes. I will truly, truly miss her! I hope you and your family have a wonderful summer."

SARA'S MOTHER CONTINUES THE STORY

Helpful People

Mr. Bayshore is really trying to help this year. He gives me hope as far as her learning disability. He's interested; he read the book I loaned him about Turner syndrome and looked up things on the Internet about her problem. He's learning about the condition, and he works with her. He is patient with Sara, which I appreciate more than anything. I always say I'm sorry that he is taken away from the other kids, because Sara takes so much of his time. But he says, "I love my job, and I like working with her, that's what I'm here for." That puts me at ease because I think sometimes she does get under people's skin, and it's frustrating if she doesn't listen to you and then does the opposite. He's trying to help her, and she's not a nuisance to him. He looks at the positive and sees little things that get better instead of waiting for the big jump, for it all to be better.

Early in the year, Mr. Bayshore requested a "staffing" because he was looking for some help with Sara. I went to that meeting, and they talked about a plan. We are all trying to use pictures to see if that helps her to stay focused and get ready for what comes next. I use them at home, too, like pictures of bedtime, cleaning up, eating dinner, and so on. We'll see if that helps her. We're doing a little bit at a time. They're just picking things they think may help.

Another person who helped was the endocrinologist; he helped me with my feelings. He helped me realize that her condition is not the end of the world. At first, when I thought about the shots, I was thrilled that maybe Sara could be fixed. I didn't know what I know now. I learned that isn't possible, but then I thought, "Great, it can be treated with growth hormones." But when he said she couldn't have kids, I took that really hard. You know, Sara gives me so much joy and to know that she couldn't have her own was devastating. Later I found out she can carry a child, just not conceive one.

The doctor let me know we were lucky to have her at all. Ninety-eight percent of the babies that are conceived with Turner syndrome don't make it to term; they miscarry.

Reading things about the condition has helped, too. I get a lot of information from the Internet. I called the Turner Syndrome Society. I talked to an adult who has Turner's. She said she is very happy and leads a normal life. She's very successful, and she graduated from college. Oh my gosh, I didn't expect Sara to even get out of high school.

Sara's father isn't dealing with it much. I tell him what I learn from the doctor appointments, and I sent him the video on how to give the shot. He read the book I loaned him, but he doesn't look into it any. I tell him she's having learning problems at school, but he says, "Well, I had them, too." He has an excuse for everything.

But Sara's stepdad has been great; he sees things in a different way. He says we don't realize how lucky we are. It could be a whole lot worse.

There are a lot of kids out there with a lot worse things than Turner's. You have to look at it that way.

The social worker at the school helped quite a bit. The shots were taking over Sara's life, so I asked that a social worker talk to her, and she did. I told her we went through a divorce a year before, and she talked to her about that. She was doing okay there, but mainly her problem was about the shots. It helped that Sara had someone else to talk to besides me. I think to be able to talk about it kind of took the pressure off for her. The social worker and I never met, but we did talk on the phone. She was very nice, very supportive.

Sara's Strengths and Challenges

Sara's a lot of fun and a good girl. Her favorite thing is making pictures. She's also getting good at writing letters, you know, but they don't make words. And she likes to read stories from the pictures; she tells her own story.

Sara plays very well with her friends. The other kids in the neighborhood like her. She likes to have her own way, but not always; I mean, she doesn't get mad if they don't do what she says. Sara has a very good imagination, very good. When she's acting with friends, she tells them what to say, and when it is two roles, she sometimes plays them both.

Her attention span is really short. Mr. Bayshore says when he reads a book aloud, she doesn't understand even 1% of it. She looks at him like she's listening, but she's out somewhere in space. He says he sees a blank look on her face. He thinks it may be a processing problem, maybe a learning disability.

At home, it's listening that we're having a difficult time with now that the new baby is here. We tell her, "Don't touch the baby's head." Then she does it anyway. It's like, I don't know which it is—does she not listen, or does she not choose to listen? She understands. When we tell her, "You're not listening," she feels bad and says, "I'm sorry."

Physically she's way behind. I had a feeling that she would be in third grade and still not be able to tie her shoes. But this year she's doing better. She buttons and zips her own coat, and tries to do her own shoes.

I think she gets frustrated with herself. I think she knows that the other kids can do things she can't. She tries to imitate others, like doing a clapping activity or something. She's always looking at someone else, but she's always a little bit behind.

At school, they're working on her understanding and following the rules. Like, Mr. Bayshore had problems with Sara playing in the bathroom with her friend. They'd be in there for 10 minutes playing with the water, laughing and having a great time. Mr. Bayshore was being consistent with her when she messed up.

She did try to pull the wool over his eyes one day, when I got a call at work and had to come take her home because she had an earache. Well, I went and picked her up, but at home she said, "Mom, this is just a trick. Go inside and get the toy out of the cereal box so I can go back to school with it." I couldn't believe it! I told her, "Sara, you can't go back to school now. When you come home sick, you can't go back." And she said, "But I have to—this is just a trick." Well, she finally realized what she did was wrong and said, "Please don't tell my teacher." She was embarrassed, but I made her tell him the next day, and he was real good with her. Mr. Bayshore explained to her that if she did that again, he might not let her go home, and she might be really sick.

I like the way Mr. Bayshore is extremely organized. He runs small groups and spends time with each group. It gives the one-on-one the children need. And he makes special time for each child. When kids walk in every morning, he gets down on his knees and says "good morning" to each one, saying their name. Sara likes that. Each child can tell him something, like "My mom and I went (someplace) . . ." He also sends home a newsletter so you know what's going to happen next week and you know what happened last week. He includes pictures of the kids in the newsletter—he's really into the kids.

Advice for Early Childhood Professionals

We asked Sara's mother if she had a few words of advice for those who might be working with a child like her daughter. After thinking about it a little, she said:

Be patient with the child, and be kind to the parent, because we don't see what's going on in school. Give the parents more information as time goes on, like a weekly report. Don't treat them any different from other families, but parents can help if they are aware of a problem. Don't wait till the report card comes out. Let the parents know right away when there's a problem, instead of trying to work on it alone. Give and accept information. Seek more information if you need more about the special condition of that child. Don't have an excuse for everything they do. Consider many different things that might be potentially the reason for problems. Be open to trying different solutions.

Epilogue

Sara is nearly 6½ years old, has completed kindergarten, and is looking forward to going to first grade.

Sara's doing much better. She's learning to do things for herself at home. She takes showers on her own and chooses her own clothes. She's a stickler about colors matching in her outfits; everything has to be exactly the same color. I mean, if she has a sweater and a turtleneck, they have to be identical.

She's also doing a lot better with her daily shots. She still has her angry phases when she whines and carries on, but she has her brave times, too.

Sara asks lots of questions about her condition, like "Why doesn't Greg [*her older brother*] have to have these shots? Why does God make me have these shots?"

In first grade we're hoping she can have an aide, and we're asking for a teacher who will give her support. I think Sara will end up being a winner out of this. There's a lot of positive in her.

INFORMATION FOR EDUCATORS ABOUT TURNER SYNDROME

Sara was found to have Turner syndrome (TS), a chromosomal abnormality that affects only females. The condition is caused by an error in the first few cell divisions of the embryo. This error causes the second X chromosome to be totally or partially missing, resulting in lack of growth hormone produced in the body. TS is thought to be a biological accident for which neither parent is responsible. It is not a hereditary condition. First described by H. H. Turner in 1938, TS occurs in one of every 2,000 female live births. An estimated 50,000 to 75,000 females in the United States have the condition.

Physical Characteristics

Turner syndrome is a condition in girls recognizable by a number of characteristics, such as short stature, lack of sexual development, arms that turn out at the elbow, webbing of the neck, and a low hairline in the back. With Turner syndrome, bones do not grow due to lack of growth hormone. The average height of a grown woman with Turner syndrome is 4 feet 8 inches. Other clinical abnormalities include puffy hands and feet, a broad chest, unusual shape and rotation of the ears, a small jaw, inner canthal folds (junction of the eyelid), arms that turn out slightly at the elbow, soft and upturned fingernails, kidney anomalies, short fingers (especially the fourth finger), a webbed neck (a stretch of membrane between the shoulder and about halfway up the sides of the neck), small brown moles on the skin, cardiac anomalies, hearing loss, and a narrow and high-arched palate (Turner Syndrome Society, 2000). Although there are many features associated with Turner syndrome, it is unusual for one child to exhibit all features; each child is unique. Some common medical conditions that occur with TS are heart, thyroid, and kidney problems; high blood pressure; heart murmur; urinary tract infections; and obesity. However, many girls don't have any significant medical problems related to the syndrome (Rieser & Underwood, 1992).

Turner syndrome is characterized by lack of sexual development and fertility, lack of breast development, lack of menstruation, and incomplete development of ovaries. Less than one percent of those with TS are able to conceive a child (Rieser & Underwood, 1992).

Health supervision guidelines have been developed by the American Academy of Pediatrics (AAP). Teens may take small amounts of estrogen in order to develop secondary sexual characteristics (AAP, 1995).

Learning Disabilities

TS does not affect general intelligence, but a tendency in some girls toward specific learning disabilities has been noted. Early reports of girls with Turner syndrome suggested that many were mentally retarded, but more recent studies say that is not true.

Girls with the condition have a tendency to have poor spatial-perceptual abilities, math weaknesses, difficulty accessing social cues, and short-term memory deficiencies. The inability to imagine objects in relation to each other can lead to problems in sense of direction and manual dexterity (Rieser & Underwood,1992; Rovet,1993). Problems with spatial relationships also make it difficult for children to deal with concepts of size, shape, or distance or to understand how parts fit together to form a whole. They can have trouble making sense of maps, charts, and diagrams, or spacing words and letters evenly when they write. Spatial difficulties may also affect the child's social behavior. Teachers have reported these children are always "in your face," talking from only a few inches away. Their inability to estimate speed and distance accurately can make them inept at games involving a ball (Smith & Strick, 1997).

Precise identification of a child's learning problems involves a comprehensive evaluation that demonstrates a significant gap between a child's potential to learn and his or her actual performance in one or more key academic areas (Smith & Strick 1997).

Hints for Success

The following suggestions may help when working with a child with Turner syndrome in an early childhood setting.

Situation 1: You have just learned that a child in your classroom has Turner syndrome. You don't know much about it, and you're wondering how much information you should share with the other children in the class.

What You Could Do to Be Helpful: Learn all you can about TS. Use the family as a resource, and get information from the list of books and articles provided later in this chapter. The family, working with its doctors, will decide how much information to give to the child and when. As her teacher, follow the child's lead in deciding how much information she wants to share with others. Allow her to explain to her peers about TS if she wishes. Be available to comfort and assure, and observe the emotional and social concerns the child may express as she becomes aware of the reality of her condition.

Answer other children's questions truthfully and matter-of-factly. Correct children's inaccurate observations, remarks, and assumptions. For example, if a child says, "She looks funny," ask the child, "What makes you think that?" Listen and provide the child with clear, simple information about what he or she is noticing. For example, "You noticed Sara is shorter than the other children. That's because she doesn't grow like other people. Her doctor gives her special medicine that helps her grow as much as she can." In addition, help the child recognize how his or her words may hurt Sara's feelings. For example, "You're curious about Sara. When you say she 'looks funny,' I'm worried that can make her feel bad. Sara wants to feel accepted and part of our group at school. Treat Sara with kindness and say things to make her feel like your friend."

Situation 2: Some of the other teachers, office staff, and children in your school treat the child with TS as though she were a much younger and less capable person because of her size. You are worried about how this affects the child's self-esteem.

What You Could Do to Be Helpful: Be a model for others by treating the child with TS according to her age, not size, in regard to expectations, responsibilities, and social activities. Help others recognize how their behavior impacts negatively on this child's self-esteem by making her feel less capable. Discuss your concerns informally, such as over lunch with colleagues, or in a more formal setting, such as a faculty meeting. Provide information about Turner syndrome, and offer suggestions of ways others can help the child develop confidence and high self-regard. Help others treat the child as an individual with potential. Point out some of the things she does well.

Situation 3: You've noticed the preschool child with TS needs assistance in managing tasks such as using the water fountain, reaching materials, or dressing for the outdoors.

   What You Could Do to Be Helpful: Arrange the physical environment so that it is comfortable and allows her the greatest independence possible. For example, provide access to classroom materials at a sufficiently low height that she doesn't have to ask for assistance. Position a footstool near shelves, the toilet, and the drinking fountain. Encourage pairs of children to help each other with dressing skills. Occasionally pair her with a less capable child so that she can be the helper. Assist her in coping with new environments, such as unfamiliar classrooms and public settings, that may be encountered. On a field trip, ask a supportive friend be her buddy.

QUESTIONS FOR DISCUSSION

1. Consider the challenges that a child of extremely short stature might have as she matures. Brainstorm a list of potential problems a child like this may face.
2. If you were this child's kindergarten teacher, what advice would you give her next year's teacher?
3. Having read this story, what are the family strengths? What parts of the story show the vulnerabilities of Sara's mom? How would you handle a parent conference with this mom?
4. How would you respond to the following remarks made by people?
   a. "She's such a baby."
   b. "You're too little to do that; I'll do it for you."
   c. "She's so tiny, what's she doing in this class?"
5. Evaluate the current early childhood setting in which you are working or volunteering. Describe what physical changes you might make to the room to accommodate a child like Sara.

RESOURCES FOR EDUCATORS AND PARENTS

Books and Videos

Hallowell, E. (1996). *When you worry about the child you love: A reassuring guide to solving your child's emotional and learning problems.* New York: Fireside.

Rieser, P. A., & Underwood, L. E. (1992). *Turner syndrome: A guide for families* (Monograph of the Turner Syndrome Society). Falls Church, VA: Human Growth Foundation.

Turner syndrome: A guide for families [Video]. (1992). Wayzata, MN: Turner Syndrome Society.

Organizations

Endocrine Society
4350 East West Highway, Suite 500
Bethesda, MD 20814-4410
Phone: (301) 941-0200
Fax: (301) 941-0259

Human Growth Foundation
7777 Leesburg Pike, Suite 202S
Box 3090
Falls Church, VA 22043
Phone: (800) 451-6434

Little People of America National Headquarters
Box 745
Lubbock, TX 79408
Phone: (800) 572-2001

Turner Syndrome Society of the United States
14450 T. C. Jester, Suite 260
Houston, TX 77014
Phone: (800) 365-9944 Fax: (832) 249-9987

Available Online

Turner Syndrome Society of the United States
www.turner-syndrome-us.org (retrieved 5/15/01)
The Website of the Turner Syndrome Society of United States provides frequently asked questions, books and other resources, chapter information by state, the opportunity to meet TS kids, a chat room, and newsgroup information.

Health Gate
www.healthgate.com/index.html (retrieved 5/15/01)
This medical research tool lists hundreds of medical publications of varying levels of medical detail. Search GENETIC ABNORMALITIES.

The Endocrine Society
www.endo-society.org/pubaffai/factshee/turner.htm (retrieved 5/19/01)
Information from the Endocrine Society.

Genetics Education Center, University of Kansas Medical Center
www.kumc.edu/gec/ (retrieved 5/18/01)
This website contains information for educators, provided by University of Kansas Medical Center, including information on Turner syndrome.

LPA Online
www.lpaonline.org (retrieved 5/18/01)
This Little People of America (LPA) Website provides information about the organization, definitions and kinds of dwarfism, and ways in which little people are successful in many walks of life.

References

American Academy of Pediatrics (AAP), Committee on Genetics. (1995). Health supervision for children with Turner Syndrome. *Pediatrics, 96,* 1166–1173.
Cunningham, P. M. (1995). *Phonics they use: Words for reading and writing.* New York: HarperCollins.
Dr. Seuss. (1954). *Horton Hears a Who.* New York: Random House.
Little People of America [LPA] (2000).
www.lpaonline.org (retrieved 5/18/01).
Rieser, P. A., & Underwood, L. E. (1992). *Turner Syndrome: A guide for families* (monograph of the Turner Syndrome Society). Falls Church, VA: Human Growth Foundation.
Rovet, J. F. (1993). The psychoeducational characteristics of children with Turner syndrome. *Journal of Learning Disabilities, 26,* 333–341.
Smith, C., & Strick, L. (1997). *Learning disabilities: A to Z, A parent's complete guide to learning disabilities from preschool to adulthood.* New York: Fireside.
Turner Syndrome Society (2000).
www.turner-syndrome-us.org (retrieved 5/15/01).

C H A P T E R   5

Marcus
Gifted and Challenging

Marcus—well, let's see. He's a really smart child, and he's a child with a really good heart. You know, he can start to think about something and tears well up in his eyes; he's thinking about something sad. That means he gets his feelings hurt, too, in the complex kind of back-and-forth of grade school boys.

Sitting in her comfortable rural dining room, Marcus's mom describes her son to us. He is currently 7½ years old, a second-grader in the local public elementary school. He's big for his age and as tall as his 9-year-old sister. From the time he was very little, Marcus's parents knew he was extremely bright.

MARCUS'S MOTHER TELLS HIS STORY

When Marcus's older sister, Tesha, was in kindergarten, her teacher sent home a questionnaire for us to fill out about giftedness. My husband and

I went to an initial meeting to introduce parents to the gifted program for first- and second-graders. The gifted teacher had all these overheads showing behaviors you look for, you know, the standard stuff: highly developed sense of humor from an early age, understanding jokes and puns really early, and so on. She told about these different characteristics; I don't remember what they all were, but we kept looking at each other, thinking about how many of those seemed to fit Marcus, who was only 3 years old at the time. They seemed to fit him almost better than they fit Tesha, who had been recommended for the program. So when it was his turn to go to school, we felt the gifted program, in which Tesha was enrolled, would be right for Marcus, too.

Recognizing Marcus's Strengths and Special Talents

Our son was very verbal, stringing words together at an early age. He walked by 10½ months, and just like that, by his first birthday, he was talking. I'm trying to remember, he might have been 2 years old when he used to tell people he wanted to be a paleontologist, a scientist who studies fossil remains. By then he was into dinosaurs, and we had a set of books and videotapes that talked a lot about them. There was a public television series that we had on videotape, and Marcus used to watch that a lot. He loved Robert Bakker, a paleontologist who appeared in the series.

Marcus's vocabulary was always advanced for his age. He would go up to complete strangers and start conversations about things. His verbal ability and his height were not very much like children his age, but his behavior was, which set him up for some difficulties along the way.

In preschool he could count things and arrange them into groups; he was really interested in doing that. And he's always been interested in building toys and in clay. One Christmas the kids got lots of fresh, colored clay from their grandma, and we put it down in the playroom. Pretty soon Marcus was bringing up all these different things he was making.

Marcus started to read when he was in kindergarten, at the age of 5. He would read signs when we went places, so I knew he hadn't memorized them because they were things he had not seen before. By 5 he was reading the dinosaur names. That was one of those things I didn't know how much weight to give to since he saw them so much and the names were attached to the pictures. I didn't know if he memorized the shape of the word or if he really did know the word. He was reading really well, but the whole reading thing fell off the rails once he had this sort of toxic relationship with school, in first grade.

Signs of Struggle

His preschool teachers, who had him 3 mornings a week, expressed some concern about his being ready for kindergarten because of the fact that he had trouble transitioning from one activity to another. If he was in the middle of something, he was in the middle of it. I had to learn to say, "Marcus, in 10 minutes you are going to have to get your clothes on and go." He'd say, "Okay, Mom." It would kind of sink in, and then in 5 minutes I'd remind him again, and he'd say, "Okay, I'll be ready." And he was usually ready when we used that technique. But to try and get him moving immediately by saying, "Okay, time to go"—that would get a lot of resistance. So we learned to use that at home the same as they did in preschool. He went to kindergarten when the others did, and that wasn't completely without incident. He really loved his kindergarten teacher, Mrs. Ortiz, who used that same warning technique.

I first realized he wasn't writing as much as the other kids in kindergarten when Mrs. Ortiz asked for a sample of Marcus's writing for his portfolio. She said, "He doesn't choose to write at school." So Marcus sat down at home and wrote a story called "The Cat Gets Blamed." It was about this cat. There was all this destruction, and when the people came home, they assumed it was the cat who had done it. But really, it was this monster that had come in and done all those things. He wrote that down and drew a picture for it, and he did a really good job of it. I had to suggest to him that it was a good idea to write down some of his stories; before that, it hadn't occurred to him.

The First-Grade Wall

We were really surprised when he hit this wall in first grade. As I said before, we thought Marcus belonged in the gifted program, but it was during the first half of first grade that we began hearing, "I hate school." I'd ask him, "Why?" He'd say, "I hate school because I'm stupid!" It was kind of circular. If he was feeling bad about being in that room, it made him feel bad about himself.

It seemed to have to do with the amount of written work he had to do. Writing was a frustration for Marcus; it has been his last and slowest area to develop, and his teacher, Miss Matthews, required a lot of writing output in the first-grade gifted program. He had all these thoughts. He was a great storyteller, but it was all verbal. Once it became evident that Marcus wasn't going to write like the others in his class, his teacher did allow him, for a while, to draw a picture and write one sentence about the picture. That was better for him.

I think the problem was not having the [*fine-motor*] skills to keep up with what was in his head, and being unable to put it on paper—that was a big frustration for him. Also, Marcus held his pencil weirdly. Lots of times I reminded him to hold it down closer to the point. He tended to hold it kind of far up. He's just now [*at age 7½*] getting to be able to control his grip with his fingers.

Since writing was a problem, the teacher suggested he try to do his writing on the computer, but he didn't have keyboarding skills either, so he was not able to keep up with his thoughts any faster on the computer. It was just as frustrating, and that didn't help.

Marcus has enough perfectionist tendencies that it really bothered him when his writing didn't tell everything about his thoughts, once he got it down on paper. And also he didn't like what his writing looked like. He'd erase a lot and redo it.

He also rejected reading at that time. Both my kids are stubborn, and both their parents are stubborn. The more the teacher tried to get him to read, when it was not something he wanted to do, the more he'd say, "No, I'm not gonna to do that!" He would literally run out of the room and stand in the hallway. I think he was trying to remove himself physically from the situation. Sometimes I was in the school building to help out, and he'd find me and say, "Mom, take me home. I don't want to be here."

Sitting still and paying attention were also hard for Marcus. For example, having his picture taken was something he didn't like because it involved waiting in line and sitting still. In kindergarten that's what happened; they brought in a photographer, and Marcus was just not dealing with that very well. He ran out of line and back to the room. Mrs. Ortiz told us he ran back to the classroom to get a little plastic horse. He held onto it in line and stayed in line. Then he got up and had his picture taken, still holding that little plastic horse. That day we learned if he had something to hold onto, he could attend to a lot of things. I noticed I listen better if I'm doing something like fiddling with this pen. We accept that in adults, but some don't want to accept that in children.

In the first-grade gifted program, we were working with Miss Matthews to let him hold something in his hand, to squish or mess with at circle times, to help him pay attention. Her initial reaction was, "No, then everybody else would have to have something, too." She was worried how she could deal with that. Later, she thought it over and decided that maybe she could allow it. It was right about then we decided Marcus should change to another school, so he didn't get to try that out.

I think Miss Matthews felt Marcus needed to just get with it. She had a lot of ground to cover with those kids, and she had 24 students. They were challenging to her because they would ask questions about everything she did, like "Why are you doing it this way?" "Why not that way?" "Oh, I have an idea . . ." Those children were hard to contain, and she just wanted it done. She expected them to do it her way the first time.

Socially, Marcus was dysfunctional enough in that class that he didn't make many friends. If Marcus wasn't getting his work done or if he did things Miss Matthews didn't like, her response was that he should just do it or he lost his recess. She probably felt she needed some leverage, but for a kid who is very active anyway, and having trouble conforming to routines, her demands were a problem. He had less opportunity to have relationships with the other kids on the playground.

A clear indication that the first-grade gifted class was not where my son was going to do well came one day when we were driving the children somewhere in the car. Marcus was in the back seat with his best friend, Jaquan, who attended a different school. I asked Jaquan how school was going. He started talking about his teacher, how she did this and said that. Then Marcus said, "My archnemesis, Miss Matthews, says _____." I thought to myself, This is not a relationship that is going to get better.

Helping Professionals Respond

Marcus started regular visits with the school social worker, Ms. Randolf, because he frequently left the gifted classroom for no apparent reason. One day she sent a note home saying Marcus had said something that she felt she needed to talk with us about. So we made an appointment with her, and at the same time I asked Marcus what he had told Ms. Randolf. He said, "I told her I thought you guys were getting a divorce." Surprised, I asked him, "Why did you tell her that?" From his response I figured out she wanted to know why he was acting up in school, and he decided to give her a reason that sounded right. But it was absolutely not true, and he knew it. He just made it up! Both of us, my husband and I, went in there. We had to sit in front of a 23-year-old social worker and explain that we were not getting a divorce and hoped she believed us. It just floored us. Everybody else in the family thought it was really funny, but at the time it wasn't funny to us.

At the end of 2 months of visits with Marcus, Ms. Randolf finally realized that Marcus was really blaming himself, thinking there was something wrong with him. He thought he was stupid and couldn't do anything right. So he'd get himself out of the room. I recognized that he'd use that same thing when we went out to dinner and he had to sit for a long time. He'd go into the bathroom two or three times, and he'd turn on the hand dryers and see how everything worked, check out the vents, and stay away.

After reading and talking to a lot of people about what we should do, we decided to make a change in his school environment. Around that same time we took him to see a child psychiatrist. Those visits resulted in Marcus being diagnosed with mild ADHD [*attention deficit/hyperactivity disorder*], with a focus on impulsive behavior. When the doctor prescribed a low dose of Aderal, my husband and I took a while to agree to try that. It was a big decision in our family, but we ended up feeling good about it. We think the medication made a difference in Marcus's life overall. He had trouble doing anything when he was on somebody else's timetable, and he needed a little help to be able to do that.

Friends and Companions Help

Marcus's cousin Shauna, who's his age, lives just around the corner. They have a strong friendship, and they play pretend a lot. They are into costumes and imagination, and my mother-in-law gave them a big box of stuff, including hats and vests. Marcus created this character he called Desert Mongo, and they'd play that. He also had an imaginary brother, Sphinx Fromage, who lived in another country with another family and they had cows. He'd tell stories about him.

Magic is Marcus's dog and companion. Marcus got Magic last year when he was having lots of trouble in school and we knew he wasn't feeling terribly unconditionally loved by us. We were having to talk with him all the time about problems. He saw another dog like Magic when he was in kindergarten. Someone brought it in for show-and-tell, and that became the question all that year: "Can I have a dog like that?" So, when I saw an ad in the paper, I said to my husband, "What do you think?" He said, "I think you're nuts, but go ahead." So we got Magic. The interesting thing to me is that Marcus has been much more responsible about taking care of his dog than I was at that age.

A Change in the School Environment

In December, when we decided that we wanted to move Marcus to a classroom where he could thrive, we had a talk with the school principal. We asked her advice, and without hesitation she suggested a well-respected teacher in another building who taught first grade. After discussing it with the other principal and the recommended first-grade teacher, Mrs. Jenson, they both agreed they would be able to accommodate our son in the class, even though it was the middle of the schoolyear. That first week I walked him into school and stayed to watch him go through the classroom door. I was worried that his relationship with school was so poor that he might not go in. Soon it was no concern.

His new teacher, Mrs. Jenson, was soft-spoken yet firm, and Marcus got off to a pretty good start. She did some things that seemed to make a difference. For example, the schedule of the day started out with a time when children could choose books and sit on the floor until everyone was settled down and they were ready to begin as a group. Pretty quickly Marcus was picking out books and wanting to read on his own. I remembered that reading had been such a struggle in the other class; this was a really positive change.

In the new classroom, he had a little chart on his desk, and he got smiley faces to keep him on track with doing his work, even if he was not necessarily doing it at the same time as the others. If he didn't do his work, he got checkmarks, and he'd bring that home to me each day. I believe she gave him a fair amount of extra time in the beginning, to overcome his fear of failure. At home, we kept track for the week. I'd say to him, "Marcus, I have to feel that I can trust you to do what you're supposed to in school." So we developed an agreement. If he ended up with more smiley faces at the end of the week than checkmarks, he could go bowling on Friday with his friend Jaquan. If he had more checkmarks, then he had to miss bowling that week. Five days was a good unit to use, just long enough for him to keep in his head. He only missed bowling 1 week, so I think the system got him cooperating and thinking there was something in it for him.

Even though things were better, there were times when school was a great frustration for him. Sometimes Marcus would be discouraged and say, "I can't do this!"—and snap, he'd break his pencil. He did this often the first few weeks in his new school. Mrs. Jenson would say, "You know, Marcus, I have other pencils, and I think you can do it." She'd encourage him to kind of get him started again.

Another good thing that happened in the spring. Mrs. Jenson mentioned to me that she was planning to loop [*move up a grade*] with the class to second grade. She wanted to know if we wanted Marcus to stay in the same class with her in second grade. When I asked Marcus what he thought of that idea—if he would like to stay with Mrs. Jenson in the fall—he said, "Yeah, I do, but I won't be in the same school next year." I said, "Yes, you'll be in the same school as you are now." He looked puzzled and replied, "No, you go someplace different every year." At that point, I realized that was what had happened to Marcus from preschool through the end of first grade—going to a new school every year. With that in mind, we felt that having the same teacher 2 years in a row would be a stability he needed. And it has been really good for Marcus and for us.

Advice for Early Childhood Professionals

Don't be so afraid of differences in kids. It isn't necessary for everything to be completely the same for everybody all the time, because kids know that life is not like that. They understand that more than some people think. If there is a way to adapt to the needs of that child, the other kids would understand.

Flexibility helps a lot. I know there's a lot of pressure on teachers to cover curriculum, and the easiest way to do that is to keep everybody on the same page all the time and all marching together so teachers have control. But there are kids for whom that is not productive. Try to be aware of times when you can be flexible in how things can be accomplished or when they are accomplished.

Allow children to use hands-on activities. Some teachers let the children use a lot of objects for learning math. That is better for our son. In general, if Marcus can be up and doing something, involving hands-on rather than just paper and pencil, he is always better off.

In the education system, a lot of emphasis is on being able to conform. I think there's a difference between a program for gifted children and one for those who are academically skilled. If children write neatly and have a big quotient of teacher-pleaser in them, they do real well in a class for academically skilled children. However, if the child is gifted but not academically skilled, such as our son, I don't think that kind of environment is right for him. The thing we said about him, from the time he was about 3 years old, is that he's probably going to do great if we can just get him through school.

Epilogue

Marcus is completing the year as a successful second-grader in the same classroom, with the same teacher. He's on a soccer team and not terrific at it, but he likes being out there with his friends. His dinosaur interest lasted until he was about 5½, and he still reads all the books. Early on he knew all the dinosaurs, could recite their names, knew what they ate, and so on. But recently that interest has been replaced by Pokemon. I was thinking about that this morning, because there are some similarities. There are about 150 Pokemon characters; they are all different, and he knows them all. They have different properties, and after they reach a certain level, they evolve. He can tell you what changes into what.

Marcus is also into building robots. He wants to make everything into robots using Legos, especially the ones that can be motorized, and anything with gears that connect. He then takes them apart. Recently at soccer he was asked to write down his hobby. He asked me, "What do you call it when you like to take things apart?" And I said, "Disassembly." He said, "Write that down, Mom. Disassembly, that's my hobby."

Marcus's life is pretty good right now. School is much better, and he's feeling good about himself. But there's still the challenge for Marcus to do things the way the teacher wants them done, which is not necessarily his way. I don't think that's going to change. I worry about the balance between challenging him enough and not frustrating him. So much of school is writing, and to some extent that is still a frustration for him. I want him to have as much knowledge as he can and be encouraged in all those ways. Yet I don't want him to get to the point where he shuts down again.

INFORMATION FOR EDUCATORS ABOUT GIFTEDNESS, FINE-MOTOR-SKILL DEVELOPMENT, AND ADHD

Giftedness

Marcus is a gifted child who was diagnosed with mild ADHD, with a focus on impulsive behavior. Giftedness is an exceptionality that is associated with cognitive development. Children are said to be gifted and talented if they display a superior intellect and/or talents that are advanced for their chronological age (Trawick-Smith, 2000). The 1988 Jacob K. Javits Gifted and Talented Students Education Act defined gifted and talented students as children who give evidence of high performance capability in areas such as intellectual, creative, artistic, or leadership capacity, or in specific academic fields, and who require special services or activities not ordinarily provided by the school (PL 100-297, Title IV, Sec. 4103). The 1993 U.S. Department of Education Report expanded the definition of giftedness to include

> children and youth with outstanding talents who perform or show the potential for performing at remarkably high levels of accomplishment when compared with others of their age, experience, or environment. They exhibit high performance capability in intellectual, creative and/or artistic areas, possess an unusual leadership capacity, or excel in specific academic fields.

They require services or activities not ordinarily provided by the schools. Outstanding talents are present in children and youth from all cultural groups, across all economic strata, and in all areas of human endeavor. (U.S. Department of Education, 1993)

The characteristics shown in Figure 5.1 are common to gifted and talented children. No child will demonstrate all of them, nor will they be evident all the time. However, a child showing a significant number of such characteristics could have exceptional potential (Education Department of Western Australia, 1997).

Fine-Motor-Skill Development

Marcus's fine-motor skills developed slowly but within a normal range of typical development. The bones of the young child's wrist do not finish calcifying and children do not gain very much dexterity in their hands until about 7 years of age. Writing requires a precision grip, which Marcus is currently developing at age 7½. Precision grip, the ability to hold the writing implement between the thumb and fingers, develops gradually and after plenty of opportunity to practice. Young children go through predictable stages in developing writing skills. The earliest state is a grasp in which only the pencil touches the page, with the arm and hand unsupported in the air. Then the little finger and elbow side of the hand are rested on the page, but the hand and fingers are moved as one unit. Finally, children learn to use their hand and fingers separately, with the hand as an anchor and the fingers moving the pencil. The final stage may not be reached until between 5 and 7 years of age (Cratty, 1986). However, because of the gifted characteristics Marcus demonstrated, his slowly developing fine-motor control was interpreted as stubbornness and poor attitude. The expectations in the gifted class placed heavy pressures on him to perform in writing, which he was physically unable to do.

Attention Deficit/Hyperactivity Disorder

Common characteristics of attention deficit/hyperactivity disorder are difficulty controlling the attention and impulses, difficulty sitting for long periods of time, and difficulty attending to tasks and following rules for quiet and impulse control (Barkley, 1998). ADHD, a condition often associated with learning disabilities, is not defined in the Individuals with Disabilities Education Act (see Chapter 10 for information on this law.) Children with ADHD demonstrate a "persistent pattern of inattention and/or hyperactivity-impulsivity that is more frequent and severe than is typically

Figure 5.1. Characteristics of gifted children.

BEHAVIOR CHARACTERISTICS	LEARNING CHARACTERISTICS
Asks probing questions that differ from classmates in depth and frequency.	Rapidly learns; understands advanced topics and follows complex directions easily.
Completes school assignments quickly; may seek further assignments or direction.	Shows insight and fantasizes about cause-effect relationships.
Lags behind peers in manual dexterity, causing frustration.	Persists in completing tasks he or she is interested in.
Sets high personal standards, tends towards perfectionism.	Sees the problem quickly and takes the initiative.
Hesitates trying things where failure is a possibility.	Learns basic skills quickly and with little practice.
Demonstrates a sense of humor; enjoys incongruities, puns, and pranks.	Is reluctant to practice skills already mastered, finds practice a waste of time.
Can have negative self-concept and suffer from poor social acceptance by age peers.	Prefers to talk rather than write; talks with speed and fluency and expression.
Daydreams and often seems lost in thought.	Can cope with more than one idea at a time.
Listens to only part of the explanation; sometimes appears to lack concentration, but usually knows what's going on.	Has strong critical thinking skills and is self-critical.
Prefers the company of older students and adults.	Surprising perceptive; constructs and handles high levels of abstraction.
When interested, becomes absorbed for long periods; may be impatient with interference or abrupt change.	Possesses extensive general knowledge and often finds classroom books superficial.
Shows unusual interest in adult issues, e.g., current affairs, justice, or the universe.	Explores wide-ranging and special interests, frequently and at great depth.

observed in individuals at a comparable level of development" (American Psychiatric Association, 1994, p. 78). ADHD, as currently conceived, actually includes three subcategories: predominantly inattentive type, predominantly hyperactive-impulsive type, and combined type. Characteristics of ADHD, while occasionally identified in preschoolers, are more commonly noticed during the primary years. Debate about what causes the disorder is ongoing. Research indicates that both biological and environmental influences are implicated. Studies of brain functioning in adults with the condition tend to confirm that they have significantly slower brain activity than adults with no ADHD. Stimulant drugs speed up brain processes and can be effective in controlling the challenging behaviors of some children with ADHD (DuPaul & Barkley, 1993). The American Psychological Association (2000) points to the need for a "thorough evaluation and diagnosis by an appropriately trained and credentialed mental health professional before a decision can be made for the child to take a psychotropic medication" (p. 3). It also indicates the need for more research to "access the long-term effects of medication, behavioral therapies, and their combinations on children" (p. 3).

Some educators and parents are concerned that ADHD is an overdiagnosed condition. In addition, they point to the decline of physical education, recess, and physical play opportunities in schools as contributing to the problem of children who are highly active.

HINTS FOR SUCCESS

Think about what it would be like to have a child like Marcus in your class. Consider the following situations that could occur and what you could do to be helpful.

Situation 1: Your kindergarten includes a child who learns extremely quickly. You wonder whether she is gifted and what you can do to provide appropriate experiences for her.

What You Could Do to Be Helpful: Learn to recognize the characteristics of giftedness. Plan ways to support the child's learning in all areas of development. Expect that some areas of development will be very advanced, while other areas may be delayed.

Situation 2: The gifted child in your first grade seems bored sometimes. He quickly completes classroom activities and wanders the room looking for something to do.

What You Could Do to Be Helpful: Create a stimulating learning environment. Arrange learning centers that have a variety of materials. For example, a literacy center might have many kinds of books, magnetic letters, magazines, crossword puzzles, word games, individual wipe-off boards, and a word wall (a strategy for teaching words that are frequently needed in reading or writing; Cunningham, 1995). Organize the daily schedule to provide time for the gifted child to investigate his own interests. Encourage the child to be curious about his interests by helping him formulate meaningful questions and responding to his ideas. At least every other day, meet with the child to review and discuss discoveries he has made. For example, if the child is interested in whales, give him time to browse informational books and pictures of various kinds of whales, make drawings, and write or dictate stories about whales. Brainstorm projects that would extend learning that the rest of the class is pursuing. For example, during a class unit on community, if others are building structures that could be a home for someone in the community, the gifted child may be intrigued to investigate ways in which a home supplies such basic needs as water or electricity and show his learning through a diagram or model.

When grouping students for small-group work, offer choices whenever possible, allowing children to choose groupmates and topics. Provide variety and offer opportunities for children to work with many different children in the class by sometimes grouping students with like interests and at other times grouping them by like complexity of assignment (Smutny, 2000).

Situation 3: The gifted child needs help carrying out activities and often seems frustrated by lack of know-how.

What You Could Do To Be Helpful: Work with the child to construct a plan, including the materials, tools, and skills needed to carry out the plan. Help gather the tools needed. Teach or find someone who can teach the child necessary skills to be successful. For example, if the child is working on producing a newspaper, you might provide paper, sample newspapers, art materials, a computer or typewriter, a copy machine, and a clipboard. You might demonstrate ways to interview interesting people, collect and illustrate data, and reproduce stories in a simple way.

Situation 4: The child who shows signs of giftedness has difficulty following your step-by-step directions, preferring to do things her own way.

What You Could Do to Be Helpful: Ask the child to discuss with you her plan to accomplish the task. If it appears that she will be able to achieve the same objectives using her own way, allow that. Help her evaluate the results.

Situation 5: The gifted child who tends to be highly impulsive is rejected by the other children because of his out-of-control behavior.

What You Could Do to Be Helpful: Observe the behavior carefully. Take notice of when and in what circumstances the child exhibits out-of-control behavior. Help the child deal with any impulsive tendencies by arranging to change the situation before it happens. Change routines slightly so that there are fewer times when this kind of behavior occurs. Take the child aside and teach alternative behaviors that are more acceptable to others. For example, "Marcus, you're excited about being in line. I'm worried when you push others around you; someone will get hurt. Stand in line with some open space around you, and keep your hands down. Let's practice what that looks like."

Situation 6: The gifted child in your classroom is seen as different from the other children and is rarely chosen as a partner for games or tasks.

What You Could Do to Be Helpful: Make it a goal to create an atmosphere of mutual respect in the class. Establish a group sharing time when children can show or talk about some work they are doing of which they are proud. Model and teach the children to use encouraging praise with each other, such as "You worked hard on that poster" or "The shark part of your story was fun." Look for a child who has at least one interest in common with the gifted child. Point that out to both of them. Encourage and help them do a project together that involves that common interest. Recognize and support creativity while building respect for the unique-thinking child through activities focusing on formulating creative ideas. For example, after introducing the concept of creative thinking, one teacher of a multi-age primary class challenged the children to come up with novel uses for a paper plate. She provided a wide array of materials to express their ideas (string, wire, felt, markers, pipe cleaners, yarn, buttons, wood scraps, and others) and tools (scissors, hole punches, glue, paper fasteners, hammer and nails, and others). The children's resulting constructions were varied, inventive, and unique. Children were praised for their unusual ideas with statements and comments and questions such as, "What made you think of that idea?"

Situation 7: A child in your first-grade class has difficulty holding a pencil and controlling it to even a small degree.

What You Could Do to Be Helpful: Offer the child many opportunities to practice strengthening the muscles in her hands through playing with clay, Play-Doh, Silly Putty, or wet sand and pounding large-headed nails into wood. Help her develop control with a pencil by offering enjoyable path-tracing activities such as mazes or dot-to-dot pictures. Help the child develop cutting skills by providing safe but sharp scissors and magazine or newspaper pictures that are interesting to the child. Offer opportunities to practice coordination through activities involving placing small pegs into peg boards, creating designs on geo-boards with rubber bands, and lots of opportunities to draw with crayons, markers, or chalk. When asking her to write, offer markers instead of pencils, as they glide along the paper and don't require pressure to make a mark on the paper. Teach the child to cross out words instead of trying to erase them. Offer alternative ways to complete written assignments, such as dictating, manipulating letters on a magnet board, or recording into a tape recorder.

QUESTIONS FOR DISCUSSION

1. What did you learn about Marcus from his mother that you might not have known if you had been his teacher? How would that information help you plan better for this child?
2. What activities were used at home that may have helped Marcus overcome his fine-motor difficulties?
3. How did Marcus's ADHD effect his success or failure at school? What strategies can a teacher use with a child with this condition?
4. What evidence did you find in the story of a stressed teacher–child relationship in the gifted class? What did that teacher do about it? Could she have acted differently? If so, how?
5. What strategies did the new first-grade teacher use to help Marcus be successful in school? What other practices could you utilize as the child's teacher, knowing his strengths and challenges?

RESOURCES FOR EDUCATORS AND PARENTS

Books and Articles

Clark, B. (1992). *Growing up gifted: Developing the potential of children at home and at school* (4th ed.). New York: Macmillan.

Ford, D. Y., & Harris, J. (1990). On discovering the hidden treasure of gifted and talented Black children. *Roeper Review, 13,* 27–32.

Gardner, H.(1983). *Frames of mind.* New York: Bantam.

Giftedness and the gifted: What's it all about? (1990). (ERIC EC Digest No. E476, Eric Document Reproduction Service No. ED 321 481). Reston, VA: ERIC Clearinghouse on Handicapped and Gifted Children.

Organizations

Council for Exceptional Children (CEC)
1920 Association Drive
Reston, VA 20191-1589
Phone: (888) 232-7733
Website: http:/www.cec.sped.org

National Association for Gifted Children (NAGC)
1707 L Street NW, Suite 550
Washington, DC 20036
Phone: (202) 785-4268
Website: http:/www.nagc.org

National Foundation for Gifted and Creative Children (NFGCC)
395 Diamond Hill Road
Warwick, RI 02886
Phone: (401) 738-0937
Website: http://www.nfgcc.org

National Research Center on the Gifted and Talented
University of Connecticut
2131 Hillside Road, U-7
Storrs, CT 06269-3007
Phone: (860) 486-4676
Fax: (860) 486-2900
Website: http://www.gifted.uconn.edu/

References

American Psychiatric Association. (1994). *Diagnostic and statistical manual of mental disorders* (4th ed.). Washington, DC: Author.
American Psychological Association. (2000, May 16). Testimony of the APA for the hearing record of the U.S. House Education and Workforce Committee on Children and Ritalin.
Barkley, R. A. (1998). *Attention deficit hyperactivity disorders: A handbook for diagnosis and treatment* (2nd ed.). New York: Guilford.
Cratty, B. J. (1986). *Perceptual and motor development in infants and children*. Upper Saddle River, NJ: Merrill/Prentice-Hall.
Cunningham, P. (1995). *Phonics they use*. New York: HarperCollins.
DuPaul, G. J., & Barkley, R. A. (1993). Behavioral contributions to pharmacotherapy: The utility of behavioral methodology in the medical treatment of children with attention deficit hyperactivity disorder. *Behavior Therapy, 24,* 47–64.

Education Department of Western Australia. (1997). Gifted and talented identification checklist. http://www.eddept.wa.edu.au (retrieved 5/19/01).

Smutny, Joan F. (2000). *Teaching young gifted children in the regular classroom* (ERIC EC Digest No. E595). Reston, VA: ERIC Clearinghouse on Handicapped and Gifted Children.

Trawick-Smith, J. W. (2000). *Early childhood development: A multi-cultural perspective*. Upper Saddle River, NJ: Prentice-Hall.

U.S. Department of Education, Office of Educational Research and Improvement. (1993). National excellence: A case for developing America's talent. http://www.ed.gov/pubs/DevTalent/part3.html (retrieved 5/19/01).

C H A P T E R   6

Irina

Learning to Have a Good Day

Mrs. Jacobs (the teacher of the "oldest group" of children at the Maple Hill Early Childhood Center) spreads several index cards on the table in front of her. Each card is an anecdotal record describing Irina's behavior during the first few weeks of school.

> *Teacher Observation, 11:30 A.M., September 21, 1999*
> Irina is outdoors in the sandpit sifting sand and making tunnels with a large metal spoon. Anthony, a 3-year-old, approaches. Without warning, Irina jumps up and shoves Anthony forcefully into the ground. (I intervene, stop the shoving and comfort Anthony). Afterwards, I ask Irina why she pushed him down. Her answer: "I don't know."

Teacher Observation, 10:30 A.M., September 29, 1999
Irina is at the "creation station" drawing with markers on paper. Marcy sits beside her. Suddenly, Irina reaches over and slashes a broad line of color over Marcy's picture. Marcy cries out, gets up, and moves to the other side of the table. Irina continues drawing.

Teacher Observation, Noon, October 1, 1999
Eugene is building a block tower. Irina walks across the block area. Without a word, she brings her fist up high above her head and smashes it down on Eugene's tower. The blocks fall. Eugene looks stunned. Irina walks on.

As we read the cards, Mrs. Jacobs says, "They're all about the same. I have many examples of Irina being aggressive toward others. She would lash out suddenly at a nearby child without any provocation. She also destroyed or disrupted other children's work. Looking back on it, I can tell you I wondered if this child could ever get through a whole day without hurting someone or damaging something."

HER TEACHER TELLS IRINA'S STORY

Irina was 5 years old when she came to my class. She had short, light brown hair and dark brown eyes. She was thin and had an angular bony appearance. Although she was a slight child, she was very wiry and very strong.

Irina lived at home with her mother, her father, and her teenage half-brother. She had a lot of contact with her grandfather, too. He lived here in town and picked her up from school most days. When her mom wasn't going to be available, she would leave me his number.

When I met her parents at the start of the schoolyear, they said Irina had been adopted when she was 2 years old. They brought her home from an orphanage in Romania. According to them, the orphanage was a pretty sterile environment where children didn't get much attention. They mostly wandered around a large room, without many toys and with nothing to do. Children had very little contact with their caregivers. Irina's parents were so glad to get her out of there—they were sure a loving home would make up for the neglect she had experienced early in life.

Her mom and I had a lot of chats at the schoolyard gate at arrival time all year long. At first, I just listened to her concerns and didn't share too many of mine. Later, it was a mutual thing, and we communicated practically every day. Irina's dad and I e-mailed back and forth—not every day, but really frequently.

From Irina's very first day in my class, I noticed that she had this real thing about water. She spent a lot of time in the bathroom playing with water in the sink. She loved the water table, too. Wherever there was water, that's where she would be. I mentioned this to her parents. They had noticed the same thing at home. Her dad had a theory about this. He said that in the orphanage the children didn't get attention from a grown-up unless they soiled themselves and needed to be cleaned up. When this happened, an attendant would take the child over to a tub with a faucet and hold the child under the water, rubbing and cleaning his or her skin. That was the only time her dad thought the children had any kind of physical contact with another person. He believed Irina associated water with love and care.

I talked with Mrs. Sylvan, Irina's teacher from last year. We're all in the same building. She said Irina had started out as a quiet child, but by the end of the year had become very aggressive. She and the assistant teacher in that room used time-outs [*removing Irina from the group for 3 to 5 minutes*] to deal with Irina's antisocial behavior toward the other children. Mrs. Sylven said she was worried that the aggression didn't seem to have any real purpose. Irina wasn't protecting herself or her things or trying to get something she wanted. As far as the teacher could tell, there was nothing the "victims" did that prompted her aggressive assaults. Irina's actions were sudden, forceful, and unexpected. Unfortunately, the time-outs didn't do much to change Irina's behavior over the course of the year.

Irina's Strengths

Irina was quite verbal and used words well to make her desires known. She talked easily about what she thought and was full of ideas.

Irina was a very creative child. She spent about 90% of the free-choice time in my classroom at the creation station making fabulous constructions. She would have some little thing in her head, and she would just go on and on with it. Some of the projects were things that she started and would work on for several days. When she got a picture in her mind about something she wanted to do, she figured out many different ways to do it.

Irina was very persistent in pursuing tasks of her own choosing. She wouldn't give up. This could last for days. For instance, there was a time when she wanted to learn how to cut a certain kind of snowflake. She just kept at it until it turned out the way she wanted it to.

She loved to play pirates. Out on the playground, she often pretended to be a pirate defending her ship. At first, she didn't interact much with the other kids, but she was quite imaginative on her own. She brought that theme indoors. Many of the things she built at the creation station were boats.

When I think of Irina, I think of a creative, determined child.

Cause for Concern

Early in the year, Irina's parents reported that she was becoming very violent at home with them. They said she hit them a lot. They told me they tried talking to her and restraining her when she did these things, but it wasn't helping much.

At school, kids were afraid of her. Her behavior was totally unpredictable. And it was very, very hurtful and violent. She would punch children hard in the stomach; she would kick them really hard, too. If she was on a climber with somebody, she might just lash out at him or her. She didn't seem angry, she just did it. As far as anybody observing could tell, there was no reason for her behavior. The child on the receiving end didn't seem to do anything other than just be there. When I would ask her why she hurt someone, she would just give me a blank look.

Irina seemed very detached from people emotionally. There wasn't much expression in her face about things. Even when her mom greeted her at the end of the day, Irina didn't smile, frown, or respond much at all.

I noticed a real lack of affect with children and other adults in the program, too. For instance, one day at the creation station, LaTesha became excited because the paint had soaked through her paper and she liked the fuzzy effect it made. She showed the painting all around. Irina was sitting right next to her and never responded in any way. She didn't so much as smile. Her face was an absolute blank. I wasn't sure whether she didn't notice, or didn't care, or didn't know how to respond. There were many incidents like that and the one described in this written record:

Teacher Observation, 11:00 A.M., October 19, 1999
   Eugene is running across the play yard. He trips over the edge of the sidewalk and falls forward on the cement. As he gets up, there is an obvious scrape on his knee and he is crying loudly. Irina is standing only a foot away. She glances over, but remains in her place. Her face registers no expression.

Insights

At first, I couldn't detect any pattern to Irina's hurtful actions. They seemed to come from out of the blue. One day I sat down and reread all my written records. I lined them up all different ways, trying to find some connections. That's when I noticed that one child in particular seemed to get more than his share of the aggression. He was a child with some developmental delays from another classroom who shared the outdoor play space with my group.

Another thing I realized was that Irina aimed a lot of hurtful behavior at younger or smaller children. From what I could tell, she was directing most of it at kids she viewed as weaker than she was. She didn't seem to hurt children who were on a par with her or who were likely to retaliate. I decided to watch for this more carefully. After a few days, it became clear that this was true.

Goals for Irina

I hoped that eventually she would be able to control herself and do what she was supposed to do and not be hurtful to other people.

My goal in the beginning of the year was to help this child be in a group of children and be accepted and be accepting of them. I hoped she could be tolerated within a group of peers and not stand out as being a problem child.

Irina's lack of empathy for others troubled me. I wished she could begin to understand that people's feelings were important and that you have to pay some attention to those things if you want to get along in the world. I didn't know whether Irina didn't feel things or whether she just didn't know how to respond. Regardless, she was so bright that I figured even if she didn't really feel empathy she could learn (from a cognitive perspective) how to act more empathic. If she could do this, she'd have an easier time mixing with the other children. I didn't want her to be a rejected child.

Establishing Boundaries

Usually in my class, if a child hurts someone or damages something, I point out how their behavior has affected others and use logical consequences that fit the situation to help children recognize the impact their behavior has on themselves and on others. I might say something like,

You're upset. It bothers me when you hit to show you're angry. Say, "I'm angry."

Or

You wanted the rolling pin. When you shoved Martha, you hurt her. Look, she's crying. Let's help her up.

Or

You didn't want Alexis to touch your blocks. Would you like it if she hit you to mean "stay away"? Let's think of another way to get her to leave your blocks alone.

None of these scripts or strategies worked with Irina. She didn't seem to care how the other children felt. And she would just give me a blank look when I asked how she felt. No amount of talking about feelings seemed to make any difference in her behavior.

When my usual strategies failed, if Irina hurt people, I'd use time-out. She didn't like time-out, but it didn't seem to make much of a dent anyway. She'd just turn around and do the same thing again. One day, about 2 months into the year, we were outside, and she did something aggressive to somebody. I said, "Okay, that's it! You're not going to play outside anymore today." I took her over to the side, and we sat together on a bench. It wasn't a time-out for just 3 minutes. I said, "We're going to sit here, and you're not playing again until it's time to go in." So we sat there for about 15 minutes until the children lined up to go indoors. I told her if she hurt anybody once we were inside, she was not going to be able to play anymore that day. I said I just couldn't have that kind of behavior in my classroom. I couldn't have somebody hurting children. She really looked at me and listened to what I was saying. That consequence seemed to help. She didn't hurt anyone for the rest of the session.

We repeated this at least three times a week for about 3 weeks, always during outdoor time. (Playground was the first thing we did each day.) She'd hurt someone, and I'd take her aside and say, "Okay, you hurt somebody—that means we are sitting." Then we'd sit on the bench together the rest of the outdoor time. That seemed to remind her about her actions, and she could get through the rest of the day okay.

Things seemed to be going better. Then one day, after we had come inside, we went over to the carpet to look at books. All of a sudden she clobbered somebody. I said, "Okay, that's it! We are out of here." I scooped her up and took her out in the hall. (My assistant took over the room.) Irina and I sat out in the hall on the floor for the rest of the morning. It was probably an hour and a half. It was a long time in the hall. But we sat there.

When her mom came, I told her what had happened. I said, "I can't have Irina in the room when she hurts other people." Her mother agreed with me. I didn't know it then, but this was a turning point for all of us.

Irina hated being out in the hall. It was boring, and she really wanted to play. It wasn't like a time-out, which was short and during which there was no talking; we talked. I just said she couldn't go back in the room. So there we were on the floor, sitting in the hall, for an hour or more.

Agreement with the Family

After 3 days, during which Irina and I spent most of free-choice time out in the hall, I told her mom that I didn't much care for it and neither did Irina. I asked, whether I could call her to take Irina home if we had more difficulties like this. Her mom said, "You bet." We talked about the importance of being together on this, and she talked to Irina's dad. We all agreed we would follow through with this limit.

After that, every day when Irina was dropped off, her mom would either give me her cell phone number or Grandpa's number so that we were able to get hold of them at any time. Irina saw us go through this each morning. It must have made an impression because we didn't need to call home until the day I wasn't at school.

I had to be out of the classroom one morning for a meeting. The day before I left, I explained to Irina that I was going to be gone. Well, the day I was away, she shoved one of the kids really hard. The assistant teacher called her grandfather. He came and picked her up and took her home. When I heard about it, I felt so sad. It seemed like we were going backwards, as I expressed in my diary entry for the day:

Teacher Diary, Wednesday, December 1, 1999
   I was out of the classroom for a meeting today. I spoke with Irina about this yesterday and told her I was going to the "big" creation station where I get lots of things for our classroom creation station and that I would try to bring back some interesting things. She seemed pleased about the prospect. Unfortunately, she pushed G hard and deliberately outdoors. When Ms. L. took her out in the hall, Irina attacked her with several severe kicks. Her grandpa was called and picked her up early. In spite of the progress we see, she is still dependent on outside forces to

keep her in check. I guess that I am that force here at school. I am very discouraged.

The day after Irina was sent home, her mom called me. She said that she arrived home just a few minutes after Irina and her grandfather got back from school. She (mom) put Irina to work, saying, "You can't go out to play and you can't watch TV; you have to do this work because you're supposed to be at school working and you're not there. So you'll just have to work at home." Mom had Irina polish silver. That night at supper, Irina said to her mom, "Thank you for fixing peas. Thank you for the good supper, Mom." Her mom couldn't get over it. That was the first time Irina had ever said "thank you."

Home and School Continue Working Together

Irina's parents and I met a couple of times. We talked about how to set limits and ways to use logical consequences. Her folks took the parenting class offered by the school. It felt pretty good working on this as a team.

Around the time we instituted the going-home strategy, Irina worked out a deal with her father that if she had a good day in school, she would get a sticker. When she earned a whole week of stickers, she would get a little surprise. That's when the idea of the skates came up.

Irina really wanted roller skates. Her father told her that if she got through a whole week at school with no hurting, she could have the skates. At the time I had mixed feelings about that. I worried, "Are we bribing this child?" Since her parents had already started it, I decided to follow through on my end. I felt we had a pact to support each other to help this little girl. We got through Thursday. Then at group time on Friday, Irina blew it. She kicked somebody—there was no apparent reason. When her mom came to pick her up, I had to say, "No, she didn't make it a whole week." Then I said, "You know, maybe you could buy the skates, but not let her use them yet." So they went off and bought the skates over the weekend. Dad took a picture of the skates for Irina to keep at school as a reminder of her goal.

Monday, Irina showed up at school with a picture of the skates. She was pretty excited about them. She had tried them on at the store, but she wasn't allowed to wear them at home until she made it a whole week without hurting anyone. She and I posted the picture on our class refrigerator. By now other children were aware of what was going on. They made friendly remarks all week, telling Irina they hoped she could earn her skates. It got to be a group thing. We all talked about what was happening. Irina showed the kids the picture of the skates. They said things like, "I hope you can get them." I said to her, "Oh, Irina, your friends are helping you. Everyone wants you to get the skates." It was the first time the children responded to her in a really positive way. We got through the whole week with no incident. Lo and behold, on Friday at dismissal time, her mom came in with the skates. Irina got up at the end of the day in front of the children, and her mom presented her with the skates. The kids all cheered for her. It was so wonderful. They were really on her side. I think it was great for her to see that they cared about her and that they were happy that she had managed to earn the skates. It was also good for them to see how hard she was trying to learn how to behave in more constructive ways.

I think the thing with the skates—the presentation and the fact that the other kids felt something for Irina—was a good thing. It caught her attention. We started seeing some more positive behavior after that.

Teaching Irina About Emotions

I read an article that said if you tell children they possess a certain quality, like being patient, they will eventually demonstrate that quality. I decided to try this in terms of emotions.

At one point I said to the staff, "It's really important to talk to Irina about feelings she might be having even if they don't seem evident." I asked them to say things to her in relevant situations like "You're happy"; "You're excited"; "You're disappointed." I thought if we kept applying feeling words to situations, if we kept telling her about typical emotions, we could give her a glimmer of what emotions might fit that circumstance. That was our affective strategy all the rest of the year.

It seemed to me that if we could help Irina figure out emotions that matched certain situations, she might become more aware of the social cues that accompany those emotions. I decided to treat this as a cognitive task, not simply an affective one. Kids found it so hard to relate to her—she was clueless about people's emotions and how her actions influenced people's feelings. I wanted to help her figure out how she could behave even if she wasn't feeling the stuff that we wanted her to feel, such as empathy for someone who was crying. In the course of our continually labeling her feelings, she started figuring things out for herself and began paying more attention to that part of people's lives.

I didn't think we could really change Irina's emotional self. Even in my wildest dreams, I didn't believe that by the end of the year she would have kids that she saw as friends, that she would be hugging people on the last day of school, that she would be saying that she was going to miss them and all that. That was totally beyond my sense of what was possible. But it all happened. We saw a real transformation in that little girl.

Signs of Progress Throughout the Year

I can't remember when the song got started. But Irina and I came up with a song that we would sing at the end of the day as I was approaching her mom or grandpa to take her to the car or meet them in the hall. It went like this: "Irina had a great day, great day, great day. / Irina had a great day all day long." (Sung to the tune of "Johnny Pounds with One Hammer.") That was the song. She really liked that a lot. She would try to sing it some days when it wasn't true. And I would say, "Not quite today." On the days it was true, we sang really loud.

Early in January, there was an incident when we were getting in line to go downstairs. One of the children said to Irina, "You're the one who hurts people." Irina put her hands on her hips and very indignantly said, "Well, I don't do that anymore!"

Later in January, Irina's mom came to pick her up and asked Irina if she wanted to walk down the stairs with her or with the other children. Irina said, "I want to walk down with my friends." My heart almost leaped out of my chest. I had never heard her refer to anyone as her friend. That was very exciting.

A real milestone happened in February with a little boy named Arthur. He spent a lot of time at the creation station, and sometimes he and Irina helped each other with their projects. Well, one day it was time to clean up. I had already given a 5-minute warning, so when I returned to the creation station, I said to Irina, "It's time to clean up; please stop now." She said, "I want one more little piece of tape." I answered, "Okay, one more, but that's all." Well, she put that one more piece on her paper, and then she said, "one more piece." I said, "No, I told you just one more. Please put your project on the shelf." She started carrying on about how she wanted the other piece of tape and asking why she couldn't have it. She kept saying, "Please, please, please let me have it." I had said "no" and wanted her to realize I meant what I said. So I stuck with it and wouldn't give her any more. Arthur, sitting nearby, had a piece of tape and gave it to Irina. She put it on her project in real triumph. Well, that made Arthur a wonderful person in her eyes. A few days later Arthur was really upset about something. He had just lost it. Ms. Turner (the assistant teacher) was taking him aside to comfort him and help him get himself back in order. He was screaming and carrying on as she was walking him to a quiet area of the room. Irina leapt out of her place at the creation station and went over and threw her arms around him and said, "Arthur, I am so sorry you have to go out in the hall." He wasn't crying because he had to go in the hall, but she thought that's why he was upset. At that moment I thought to myself, "Boy, this kid has just displayed some empathy for another human being." I was so excited that day, I cannot tell you.

One afternoon in March, I realized I was in the room and I didn't know where Irina was. It was the first time that year that I didn't know where that child was every minute of the day, and it was all right.

And then this really cool thing happened. Late in May, we were getting ready to gather for our last circle time of the day. A dad had come in partway through the session to help in the classroom. Irina hadn't even noticed him come in. Eventually she saw him sitting on the floor with his son on his lap. She walked over and said, "Are you his daddy?" He answered, "Yes, I am. I got to come and help with the library today." She asked, "How did you feel when he was born?" That was the first time I had heard her verbalize to another person about the possibility of having feelings. The dad said he was very happy. He was glad that he had three sons and Eugene was his third son. I was very encouraged by her awareness and the interest in others that this question demonstrated. This was the first time that she had asked anyone how he or she felt about anything. I would have been surprised if *any* of my children had come up with something like that. But with Irina, it blew me away.

I guess Irina was most dependent on me during the first several months as the authority figure at school. Over time, her dependence on me lessened. She got so she trusted other people to help her maintain control. By the end of the year, she got to the point where most of time she could control herself. I'm not saying we didn't have more aggressive behavior from her, but it wasn't the hostile aggression we had seen earlier. When she wanted something, she'd grab it, or if somebody did something she didn't like, she'd push, but it wasn't a sock in the gut that knocked them over. The number of unprovoked attacks steadily decreased. By May, we hardly saw any at all.

Final Thoughts

It was a gratifying year. I had no idea at the beginning that we would see the progress that we did. Although I felt Irina had gotten over a huge hump, I knew there was a lot more she needed to work on socially. I expressed these thoughts about Irina's future in my diary.

Teacher Diary, July 10, 2000
Irina is enrolled in the morning session of a public school kindergarten in our community. Her mom called to say Mrs.

Franklin was her assigned teacher. I am so pleased. Mrs. Franklin has a good reputation in the district. She is gentle but firm and very child-centered. I think she's an excellent choice for Irina. During our conversation, I told Irina's mother that I would be happy to talk with the kindergarten teacher about some of the strategies we had used over the year. Consistency will be an important issue for Irina as she makes the transition to her new school.

Teacher Diary, September 12, 2000
Irina came back for a visit today. She ran right up to me and gave me a hug. A year ago, such an obvious display of emotion would have been unthinkable!

Epilogue

I greatly feared that our success with Irina's behavior would be misinterpreted by her parents to mean that she was somehow "cured" and didn't need continued support or intervention. Unfortunately my fears were realized, as I recorded in my diary:

Teacher Diary, October 21, 2000
I bumped into Irina's mom at Wal-Mart today. Kindergarten is not going well. Irina's aggression is mostly in check, but she isn't cooperating with the teacher and she continues to have a hard time "reading" other people's social cues. Apparently she laughed when a child got hurt the other day. Also, she has teamed up with another child to disrupt the class in many ways. I mentioned that I hadn't heard anything from Mrs. Franklin and that I would be happy to meet with her to talk about the coaching strategies we began last year. I was surprised when Irina's mom said they had never mentioned my offer to the teacher. In fact, they haven't told the teacher about Irina's pre-primary experiences at all. Her parents don't want Irina targeted for special education. Her mom said they hoped that last year's problems were over and that Irina could just go to school like everybody else.

Teacher Diary, December 14, 2000
Irina has been referred to the intermediate school district for assessment. Mrs. Franklin says they are exploring the idea that Irina may be demonstrating some form of emotional impairment such as attachment disorder or conduct disorder. The school is suggesting that Irina spend part of each day in a program for

emotionally impaired children. I worry that if they put her in a whole room of emotionally impaired kids that we will lose her. If all the kids are exhibiting inappropriate behavior, she might try to outdo them, and she could be very successful at that!

INFORMATION FOR EDUCATORS ABOUT EMOTIONAL/BEHAVIORAL DISORDERS

Young children enter kindergarten with much to discover about the social world. Even youngsters who have had the benefit of previous early childhood program experience are just learning how to behave in school and how to get along with their peers. At one time or another, most youngsters this age break rules, misbehave, or get into disagreements with classmates. However, for some children, hurting others and poor social skills are such chronic problems that they interfere with their learning and seriously compromise their ability to form constructive relationships with others. The assessment team at Irina's elementary school is exploring the possibility that Irina may be a child whose social problems fall within the classification of emotional/behavioral disorders.

Definitions

Two definitions are guiding the assessment team's deliberations. The first is found in the Individuals with Disabilities Education Act of 1997. Under this definition, children may have an emotional/behavioral disorder if they are unable to build or maintain satisfactory interpersonal relationships with peers and teachers, if they display behaviors or feelings that are atypical under normal circumstances, if they are generally unhappy or depressed, or if they develop physical symptoms or fears associated with personal or school problems.

Professionals who belong to the Mental Health and Special Education Coalition (MHSEC) have expanded this definition. They indicate (Turnbull, Turnbull, Shank, & Leal, 1999) that the term *emotional or behavioral disorder* means a disability that is

(i)   characterized by behavioral or emotional traits so different from appropriate age, cultural, or ethnic norms that the responses adversely affect educational performance, including academic, social vocational or personal skills;

(ii) more than a temporary, expected response to stressful events in the environment;

(iii)   consistently exhibited in two different settings, at least one of which is the school;

(iv)   unresponsive to direct intervention applied in general education or the condition of a child such that general education interventions would be insufficient. (pp. 175–176)

States and local school districts vary widely in their interpretation of these definitions as well as in the terms they use to describe children whose behaviors are encompassed by them (Turnbull et al., 1999). Generally speaking, however, the term *emotional and behavioral disorders* applies to attachment disorder, anxiety disorder, bipolar disorder, oppositional-defiant disorder, conduct disorder, eating disorder (anorexia nervosa and bulimia nervosa), and childhood schizophrenia.

Approximately 8.1 million children in the United States, almost 15% of the younger generation, exhibit some form of emotional/behavioral disturbance (Council for Exceptional Children, 2000). Although the causes of such disorders are not fully understood, some factors include genetics, physical injury, infection, and brain damage before and after birth, as well as poverty, child abuse, and neglect. Recent studies show that children whose caregivers are alcohol or substance abusers, or have had any other mental illness, are also vulnerable. Exposure to violence, harsh methods of discipline, and deprivation are additional factors that may contribute to children's emotional/behavioral disorders.

The warning signs of emotional/behavioral disorders are not always obvious and usually develop gradually. All children express anger, fear, sadness, withdrawal, or opposition to authority, but the child with an emotional/behavioral disturbance displays negative behavior and emotions with greater intensity, more often, and with less provocation.

Behavioral Characteristics

Emotional/behavioral disorders manifest themselves in two different ways (University of Kentucky, 2000). Some children exhibit internalized problems such as

Depression
Withdrawal
Excessive shyness
Decreased interest in activities
Anxiousness
Low energy

Other youngsters have more externalized problems, including

> Recurring patterns of aggression toward people and objects
> Noncompliance with reasonable requests
> Tantrums
> Acting-out behaviors
> Persistent lying or stealing
> Excessive arguing

The presence of any one of these behaviors alone does not constitute an emotional/behavioral disorder. As pointed out earlier, all children have emotional/behavioral problems sometimes; it is the persistence, severity, and resistance of the behavior to change that helps to determine whether or not it is classified as a disorder (Kostelnik, Whiren, Soderman, Stein, & Gregory, 2002).

Hints for Success

Young children have a lot to learn. How to express themselves and how to get what they want without hurting others are prime lessons. As an early childhood professional, you will work with numerous children whose behavior is aggressive and who have difficulty developing constructive relationships with others. Some of the children you encounter may be classified as having an emotional/behavioral disorder; most will not. In addition to strategies highlighted by Irina's teacher and parents, here are some strategies professionals find effective when children act aggressively in the classroom.

1. Model nonaggressive behavior yourself. Even when confronting children whose behavior angers or frustrates you, keep your voice low and your movements controlled. Do not scream or make threatening gestures.
2. Provide children with opportunities to feel competent. Assign children age-appropriate responsibilities, such as taking the clean-up sign around, feeding the fish, or collecting the journals. Give children chances to make choices and to try a variety of tasks and experiences independently. Structure these so that children feel challenged but not so overwhelmed that success is unlikely. Teach children the skills they need to achieve their goals, such as how to use tools, how to play games, or how to work with a partner.
3. Help children learn assertive language. Do this with the child who engages in hurtful behavior and with those who are victims. Plan dis-

cussions and create activities to highlight sample words children might use when they want to express themselves or maintain their rights assertively. Take advantage of teachable moments to address these same lessons. Sample scripts include: "No hitting." "Ow, that hurt. Don't hit me." "I'm still using this." "You can help me put this back together." "When will I know your turn is over?" "Stop."

4. Set consistent limits on children's aggressive behavior. When a child hits or pushes another child, stop the aggressive action immediately. Use physical intervention if necessary. Acknowledge the aggressor's aim (if that's discernible); for example, "You wanted a turn with the computer." If it is not obvious, express your concern and explain why the hurtful action is unacceptable. For children who are nonverbal or very young, suggest specific alternate actions to the aggression. Help older, more verbal children generate their own ideas for a solution to the problem. Clearly state the consequences for continued aggression. Follow through immediately if children persist.

5. Help aggressive children recognize how their actions affect others. Point out cues to help them recognize how other people feel. "When you knocked Jerome's blocks down, he got upset. Look at his face. He is really sad."

6. Attend to the victims of aggression. Comfort the victim in front of the aggressor. Involve the aggressor in helping the victim (by rebuilding the block tower, for example, or getting an ice cube to put on a bumped head).

7. Make it clear that aggression will not be tolerated in your classroom. Tell the aggressor directly, "I cannot let you hurt people in this room." If a child hurts you, react strongly: "OW, THAT HURTS!"

8. Look for patterns that contribute to children's aggressive behaviors. Is there some consistency in the time of day when the aggression happens? Is there a pattern in who the victims are or in what children and adults are doing? Does the aggression occur during certain routines or in a particular place? Make changes in the environment, routines, or schedule as necessary to avoid "problem" situations.

9. Reward children for engaging in nonaggressive behavior. Find times when the child who is often aggressive is behaving appropriately. Point this out to the child and to others, so everyone recognizes that the child is capable of positive actions, too.

10. If a child's behavior is more extreme than you believe you can cope with on your own, get help. Sometimes someone outside your own setting can be more objective about the situation or provide insights you might not generate on your own. Invite another teacher or administrator to observe the situation for a while and offer suggestions.

1. Make a list of all the strategies the teacher and Irina's parents used to support Irina. Which of these were similar to ones you have learned about in your training? What new strategies did you encounter in this chapter?
2. What lessons have you learned from Irina's story?
3. Edward Hallowell (1999) said, "We must learn to recognize the signs of emotional or behavioral disorders so that we don't treat them as simply diseases of the will, moral failings on our children's part, or parental failings" (p. 5). What do you think he meant by this statement, and how might this apply to Irina's story?
4. How would you respond to the parents of one of Irina's victims who complained to you about Irina?
5. Consider what is happening to Irina in her kindergarten class as described at the end of this story. How do you perceive this situation? In retrospect, what changes might the adults have made in their behavior to better support Irina's positive development?

RESOURCES FOR EDUCATORS AND PARENTS

Books and Journals

Council for Exceptional Children. (1991). *Working with behavioral disorders: Mini library*. Reston, VA: Author.

Henley, M. (1997). *Teaching self-control: A curriculum for responsible behavior*. Bloomington, IN: National Education Service.

Behavior Disorders
Available through the Council for Children with Behavior Disorders on a quarterly basis. Feature articles report research.

Beyond Behavior
Available through the Council for Children with Behavior Disorders. Feature articles focus on translating research and describing practical strategies for working with children with behavior disorders.

Organizations

Center for Mental Health Services (CMHS)
5600 Fishers Lane

Room 17-99
Rockville, MD 20857
Phone: (703) 684-7722
Fax: (703) 684-5968
E-mail: childinfo@nmha.org
This is a division of the National Mental Health Association, which is actively engaged in public education, advocacy, and coalition-building efforts. The CMHS focuses primarily on mental health issues of children, youth, and families.

Council for Children with Behavioral Disorders
c/o Council for Exceptional Children
1920 Association Drive
Reston, VA 20191-1589
Phone: (888) 232-7733, (703) 620-3660
TTY (text only): (703) 264-9446
Fax: (703) 264-9494
E-mail: cec@cec.sped.org
WebSite: http://www.cec.sped.org

REFERENCES

Council for Exceptional Children. (2000). Behavior Problems in Young Children. http://www.cec.sped.org (retrieved 5/18/01).

Hallowell, E. M. (1999). *Connect*. New York: Pantheon.

Kostelnik, M. J., Whiren, W. P., Soderman, A. K. , Stein, L. S., & Gregory, K. (2002). *Guiding children's social development* (4th ed.). Albany, NY: Delmar.

Turnbull, A., Turnbull, R., Shank, M., & Leal, D. (1999). *Exceptional lives: Special education in today's schools*. Upper Saddle River, NJ: Merrill.

University of Kentucky. (2000). Children with Behavior Disorders. http://www.uky.edu (retrieved 5/18/01).

CHAPTER 7

Sam

A Complex Child

Elusive is the word that comes to mind when people talk about Sam. His special needs are not apparent immediately. But the more you interact with him, the more you get a sense that something is awry.

This is Sam's story, told by two people who care about him deeply, his mother and his kindergarten teacher. Together they will help us gain a better understanding of this very special child.

SAM'S MOTHER BEGINS HIS STORY

"It's a boy!" Sam was born 7 years ago. He is the oldest of our three children and the first grandson in a family of all daughters and granddaughters. It was a big thing that we had a boy. He was such a wonderful baby. We were thrilled.

Sam had his first seizure when he was 3½ months old. We were in the Bahamas on vacation, and Sam had a little cold. His crib was next to our bed. Suddenly, in the middle of the night, we heard these strange sounds; he was having a seizure. It lasted for hours. There was no ambulance, so we took a taxi to the hospital. He was seizing the whole time. Once we got there, it was hard for the doctors to find a vein. He needed an injection to stop the seizures. It was so chaotic. He had to stay in the hospital 3 days and 3 nights.

When we got back to the United States we had him evaluated. They said he might have a seizure disorder, but they didn't know why. They said we should wait to see whether he needed medication. At 6 months of age, he had another long seizure. We lived in the countryside and had to be "med-evaced" in a helicopter to the nearest hospital. Maybe you can imagine how we felt. It was a nightmare.

After that, he went on medication. He has remained on it ever since, and it has helped a lot. Now he only has seizures when he is sick or is getting sick. Sometimes they happen when he is overly tired.

Being sick is what started the trouble when he was 2. He had an ear infection, with a high fever. This led to a seizure on Thursday. We went to the hospital, and they sent us home without any additional medication, saying the seizure was an outcome of his being sick. On Saturday we went to a pediatrician, and he gave us another antibiotic for the ear infection. That night Sam seized for hours and had to be incubated. It was the most traumatic seizure experience he had ever had. They gave him Valium to calm his nervous system, and then he wouldn't wake up. We knew something was really wrong. It was Sunday; our doctor wasn't on call; we had to deal with another pediatrician. He kept saying Sam would be fine; he just needed to sleep off the Valium. He didn't check for anything else. So for 36 hours Sam went undiagnosed with bacterial meningitis [an infection or inflammation of the meninges, thin membranes that cover the brain and spinal cord].

They didn't know about the meningitis until Sam started going into toxic shock on Monday. He was in a coma for a week. Eventually, he had to have neurosurgery because there was pressure on his brain. My sister, my mother, my husband, and I took shifts being with him. At the time, I thought we were there in case he woke up. But I realize now we were really there in case he died.

Every hour Sam went undiagnosed for the meningitis was critical time lost. There might have been a big difference in how things turned out if the doctor had treated it right away. I know many parents who don't know why their child has special needs. I don't know if that would be better or worse for us.

Unfortunately, we know that Sam's brain was damaged as a result of the meningitis and there is no way to go back—no way to change it. That's a very hard thing to accept. It took us 3 years until we actually talked about it with the pediatrician who saw him that weekend. We had a meeting in his office, and he told me how guilty he felt every single day. I forgave him and told him that medicine is not only a science, but also an art. He said this changed his life. I said, "It changed our lives, too." I can't blame him for not catching it, but you know there are times when I do feel so sad about it all, when I think of how different life might have been for Sam and for me and for everyone in our family.

Some kids who get bacterial meningitis at that age die. And if they do live, there's a good chance they'll become deaf. We're lucky. Sam lived! He has no hearing impairment at all. He's a miracle child.

It's been 5 years since all that happened, and the doctors say it has taken all this time for Sam's central nervous system to calm down. His brain is healing still, but there is scar tissue on parts of his brain that will never go away.

Sam's Wonderful Qualities

Sam is a physically beautiful child—curly hair and usually a happy smile. [*See Figure 7.1 for Sam's self-portrait at age 7.*]

He is the sweetest person. Everyone who knows Sam describes him as sweet. There's something about him—a certain charm that people are drawn toward. He knows how to win people's hearts, especially grown-ups. He gets right into your heart. It's a very special quality.

Sam has such strong empathy for people who are hurt, sick, or crying. He's fascinated by anybody who has special needs—fascinated. He immediately notices people who use walkers or people who are deaf.

Sam is tremendously imaginative. He spends hours pretending.

Sam has a photographic memory. Let's say you read him a book 3 years ago; he can remember every word. He can tell you when you're reading it wrong or if you skipped a part, even if he only heard it once. That's a great strength for learning, and it has helped him quite a bit.

Figure 7.1. Sam's self-portrait.

Sam's Limitations

Sometimes Sam says, "My mind gets all turned around." That's what he says, and that's what it feels like, I guess. He lacks the kind of processing skills you need when you are learning and thinking. It's hard for him to solve problems; he gets easily frustrated and then he cries.

He has so much information coming in all the time. He hears and sees everything. When he goes down the hall to go outside, he's going to notice many things that you don't. That's a strength—and a hindrance sometimes. It can be hard for him to focus. When he does get focused, he often gets stuck on one thing and has a hard time switching gears.

Sam's fine-motor skills have been wiped out. I buy pants and shirts that don't have buttons, snaps, or zippers so he won't have to deal with it all the time. He's probably never going to write; he can barely write his name. This year we're going to use a computer to help him.

The doctor told us that kids with Sam's kind of problem often become aggressive or anxious. He is a little bit of both, but he's more on the anxious side, which I guess I'm happy about. I'd rather he was anxious than always hurting people. He gets anxious when he can't do things. His anxiety is the kind of thing we've been told we will eventually be able to treat with drugs.

Controlling Sam's Seizures

Sam takes a variety of medications. He's had intensive occupational and speech therapy since he was 2. We do music therapy, and right now we are also doing cranial manipulation. This is a hands-on technique, performed by a trained therapist. The therapist gently manipulates the bones of Sam's head, spine, and pelvis. In the process, she also massages the surrounding membranes and stimulates the cerebrospinal fluid. This has been our most unconventional treatment with him, but we're willing to try whatever might help.

Sam goes to bed each night by 7:00 or 7:30 P.M. He needs a lot of sleep because his energy level is so low. It's partly due to his medication and partly a result of the brain trauma. Some days he still needs a nap.

We have a very structured environment at home. We follow the same routines faithfully every day. This makes things easier for Sam and helps with his feelings of anxiety.

Effect on Sam's Parents

The meningitis was the most indelible experience I ever had. Both my husband and I agree that it is the defining thing in our lives. There is a lot of trauma connected with having your child get something very normal like a germ running around in his ear and then having that lead to something that will never heal. Both of us (my husband and I) have worked on it in therapy; we've had to because it's so traumatic. I'll never be a regular mother again.

Timmy, my middle child, recently got quite sick, and I couldn't help but think, "My child is sick; now he's going to die." That was my immediate response; it was not conscious, it was not cognitive—it was purely emotional. That kind of feeling just never goes away.

My husband and I decided to have another baby right around the time Sam got meningitis. I took a pregnancy test while Sam was in the hospital and found out I was pregnant. So it's a gift that we had Timmy. I couldn't have done it (had another baby) for years and years had we known that things were going to turn out for Sam the way they did. I would have been afraid.

We have three children now, and my husband wants four. It's nice because it normalizes everything. Sam has to share with other kids. The world does not revolve around him alone. Even though the boys fight like cats and dogs, they're good for each other.

There have been so many people who have helped us. We've been very lucky, but I also know that we're good at making connections. I search and search until I find what we need. When we first moved here, I had to find a private occupational therapist who also specialized in sensory integration. It was really hard to find the right person, but eventually I did.

Family Reactions

My younger sister is my best friend. She's validating, but not excessively so. She never makes me feel stupid or like our concerns about Sam make things inconvenient. She's just perfect the way she is. I don't know why other people can't be like that.

There is a real lack of empathy that goes on with my other sisters. That's a big stressor. They think we're being too inflexible and wonder what's wrong with us. They don't understand why we're not willing to do a lot of things that to them seem like no big deal—like letting Sam stay up late.

With my husband's family, the whole thing with Sam has been a bonding experience. His parents are doctors. This situation has given us a lot of things to talk about and different ways for them to help us. They have helped us a lot (with information, support, and contacts in the medical community).

Reactions from Friends

When you have a child with special needs, some of your friends feel like they can't understand what you're going through because their family never had a situation like the one you are experiencing. That is a barrier. Another reaction is, "What are you talking about? There is nothing wrong with your child. Why are you acting this way?" So it goes to either extreme.

There have been some families who have embraced all of us, and that has been so wonderful. They like us and they "get" Sam. They are the only kind of people we can be around and really be comfortable with. There's no judging, no second-guessing, no trivializing, and no making a big fuss. We feel accepted and normal.

A Special Student Teacher

There was a student teacher from Sam's kindergarten who stayed with my kids when I had Jonathan, my third child. She had such a beautiful outlook on all of my children, but the way she was with Sam was just amazing. She thought Sam was a wonderful person. She believed in him in a big way and treated him in a normal fashion. Whenever she was with him, you could tell she liked him, and that meant a lot to my husband and me.

Advice for Early Childhood Professionals

1. *Listen to what parents have to say.* They know their child best. They know what is typical and what is not typical for that particular child. This knowledge goes beyond the child's "condition."
2. *Have a meeting ahead of time with the parents.* I talk to Sam's teachers about Sam's seizure medicine and the fact that they need to call 911 if he has a seizure in school. However, I don't talk only about the life–threatening stuff. I also tell his teachers how he learns and his history. I don't think you can work with Sam very well without knowing all of that.
3. *Find ways to communicate with the family on a regular basis.* Make sure the communication is two-way. It's been so wonderful to have a little notebook that goes back and forth between home and school. His kindergarten teacher wrote to us almost every day. Now we do that with his paraprofessional aide, too.
4. *Treat parents as partners in the education process.* I don't see how you can be successful with a child without working together. For example, last year Sam had some problems listening to his resource room teacher. At first Sam had no difficulties in her room, and then all of a sudden he got somewhat defiant. He didn't want to cooperate or do

what she asked him to do. She didn't tell me at first. When she finally did, we had a strong talk with him because he did something wrong. It wasn't like he hit anyone, but school is a high priority with us, and we wanted him to pay attention to his teacher. He did better when we were all working on it together.

5. *If the child comes to you with a certain label, remain open-minded and see beyond the label.* First, get as much information you can about a child's condition. Then think outside the label. Nobody is just a label, and even kids who have the same label are all different.

6. *It is important to have high expectations.* So many people I have come across just don't think children with special needs can do things. I'm not just talking about academics. I mean social expectations, emotional expectations, and physical expectations, too. Kids like Sam can learn.

Sam entered a half-day private kindergarten program at age 6. His class had 20 children, a teacher, an aide, and a student intern. Sam received services from an occupational therapist and a speech therapist throughout the year. He had been to preschool before and made an easy transition from home to kindergarten. Sam's teacher, Ms. Kaminski, provides these observations about his kindergarten year.

SAM'S KINDERGARTEN TEACHER TELLS ABOUT HIS PROGRESS

I thoroughly enjoyed having Sam in my classroom; he was a bright child and very sweet. It was hard to tell at first that he had any problems. His intelligence, his language, his charm, and his social skills masked them.

At the home visit I learned about Sam's seizure disorder and also about the results of the meningitis. Sam never had a seizure at school, but he had several at home during the year.

Sam had highly developed verbal skills and an excellent verbal memory. One time the children were dictating stories. Sam dictated a long involved story about a rabbit. I recognized it as *The Run Away Bunny*. We had been sitting near a framed illustration taken from that storybook. Looking at the picture must have triggered his memory, and he dictated the whole thing from start to finish. He could do that. He could repeat verbatim a book I had just read. He enjoyed stories and loved books.

Sam's language sounded very mature, but also scripted. I realized over time that he used books as a language model. Often he used expressions he had heard in stories as part of his ongoing conversation. Sam talked a lot and was very imaginative. He liked to pretend.

Sam was a pleasant child in the classroom. He was able to express his feelings in words and had pretty good self-control. Once he learned our classroom rules, he was able to follow them without much difficulty. For instance, Sam loved whistles. He has a whole collection of whistles and would often show up with a whistle around his neck, in his bag, or attached to his jacket. I use a whistle on the playground to let the children know when it is time to come in. I explained to him that the rule at school was that the whistle meant come in and get in line, and if he was going around the playground blowing his whistle, it could be very confusing for the other children. I asked him not to blow his whistle during recess. I had to explain it a couple of times, but he really got good at following that rule. When it was time to come in, often I would say, "Okay, Sam, now you can blow your whistle and let everyone know it's time to come inside." Then he'd blow his whistle and we'd troop inside.

Supporting Sam's Development

Physical Development

Sam's occupational therapist told his mom and me that Sam didn't have much "motor memory." She said almost every time he performed a motor task, it was like he was learning it for the first time. This was true for both gross-motor and fine-motor skills.

Sam was okay at walking, and he could run a little. However, he had really poor muscle tone. When we did activities that involved sitting on the floor, I had to have an adult sit next to him so he had someone to lean on while he was sitting and someone to push on when he had to get back up. Sometimes, without the right support, he simply fell to the floor in a heap.

Our classroom was on the second floor. I don't think it was easy for Sam to trudge upstairs every day. I mean, he did it, but sometimes he was tired. He would wait and get in at the end of the line and hold onto the rail or someone's hand. He had quite a workout by the time he reached the top.

We did a lot to encourage Sam to try some of the gross-motor equipment outdoors, like getting on the slide or trying the climber. By the end of the year, he had made great strides in this regard.

His mom couldn't get out much with her last pregnancy, so we had a notebook that went back and forth. I would write in it almost every day, and she would write in it sometimes, too, just to share things that had gone on either at home or at school. This way she could have something to talk about with Sam at home, for instance, whom he had played with and what he had done. It also gave us insights into things that were going on that might have affected his concentration or his willingness to cooperate. [*See Figure 7.2 for some examples of notebook entries by Sam's teacher describing his gross-motor experiences.*]

Sam was a bright little boy. He knew how he wanted things to look when he was drawing. Because of his poorly developed fine-motor skills, he couldn't draw something like it was supposed to be in his mind, and that was very hard for him. He got discouraged when he tried really hard and the results were not what he thought they should be.

One way we addressed the fine-motor area was to give him a variety of things to manipulate. Buttons for dress-up clothes and paper to tear worked well. We gave him chalk to use for drawing on the sidewalk, and he liked that.

We made sure to recognize small steps as he completed them, rather than waiting for him to accomplish a whole task at one time. For example, breaking things down into smaller steps helped him a lot when he was learning to use scissors or when he tried to do things like pattern blocks.

Social Development

When Sam came to kindergarten, he was really good at interacting with adults. He needed more support interacting with kids. At first he didn't know how to break into a group that was already playing. I gave him sample scripts to help with this (e.g., "I could be the dinosaur looking for eggs." "I'd like a turn next."). Another thing I did was to invite other children to play with the two of us together. Once the playing got started, I faded out.

Sometimes Sam didn't recognize that other children wanted to play or that peers were acting in friendly ways. I purposely drew his attention to the children he played with and to the positive interactions he had with peers. Sometimes, it seemed he didn't notice. He'd say, "Oh, yeah," after I brought things like that to his attention.

As I said before, Sam loved to pretend. At times he had a hard time recognizing that other children might have good ideas for make-believe. He was happiest if he could just take over and assign everybody to what they were supposed to do. Not all the kids were receptive to that all the time. Helping him to be more accepting of the other children's ideas was something we worked on throughout the year. [*See Figure 7.3 for descriptions of interactions Sam had with peers in the classroom.*]

Figure 7.2. Teacher's entries in notebook sent to his parents about Sam's gross motor experiences.

September 6	I am noticing that Sam spends most of outdoor time talking to adults. We will work on getting him to be more active.
October 10	Allison asked Sam if he wanted to ride on the back seat of our two-seat trike. He said "yes!" It's the first time he has gotten involved in a gross-motor activity. Even though he was just riding, he had to get up and down and crunch his legs to fit in—that's a start. Plus, he had fun!
February 8	Sam began, with help, to climb up to the top of the twirly slide and to slide down. He told me he was scared, and then he slid down. He repeated this twice.
March 16	Sam offered Erik a ride on the back of the two-seat trike. That was a real challenge for him—to have the strength to pedal the trike with someone else on the back. He made it almost the whole way around.
April 8	I am so excited! We just came in from the playground. Sir Cyclone (Sam) was with me for a while and climbed up and slid down all the slides on the playground as he attempted to escape from King Smudge (Erik). The most exciting part was the long tunnel slide, which is reached via the circle climber. I talked/coached/guided Sam up the first time. I stood nearby and did the same verbal coaching the next three times, but I never put a supporting hand on him! Later, on his own, he went down the tunnel slide, approaching when three other children were on it. I am thrilled. He remembered where he had to turn his body and duck his head.
May 22	Today Sam climbed to the top of the tube slide—on the outside of the tube! Ms. Stuben was behind him, verbally coaching. Sam did it all the way. The biggest hurdle was climbing over to the platform at the top. Your boy is getting physical. I am so pleased.

Figure 7.3. Sam engages in friendly peer play, as explained by his teacher in the notebook sent to his parents.

February 1	At small-group time, we were trying to fit pattern blocks into rather abstract forms. Sam didn't think he could/would do them, but he was very pleased to announce "I did it!" after each of the three that he completed. Mike supported this with a "Good work, Sam."
February 10	Lisa was an oviraptor on the playground. Sam was several kinds of dinosaurs trying to save his eggs. They enjoyed pretending together.
February 22	Sam spent time in the book area with two children. I pointed out to Sam that he was playing with Kyle and Mike. He was pleased. It seems he needs help to notice.
March 16	Outdoors, Patrick called through the fence, "I love you, Sam." Sam responded, "I know."
April 21	If Sam sings his newest song for you, don't be surprised! We were in the gym. Jerome has taught him a little ditty called "Batman Smells" (tune of "Jingle Bells"). They had a fine time.
April 22	At center time, Trevor had been busy making a snake out of clay and bits of wood. Sam wanted one and asked Ms. Stuben to make it. She suggested that he ask Trevor to help him. Trevor readily agreed, started a snake, and gave it to Sam. Sam wanted someone else to do it all, but eventually he did connect some wood bits to it—it was hard work for him, but he did it. Eventually he had a satisfactory snake. He and Trevor carried it around and announced, "It's not a bad snake, just misunderstood!"
May 11	Outside Sam and Trevor are searching for "Boris," he's a (pretend) lost Russian wolfhound whom they love very much. He's really special because he can talk on the telephone, but he's not choosing to answer today.

Cognitive Development

Number activities, counting, and patterning tasks were very challenging for Sam. Anything involving strategy was very difficult. He would get quickly frustrated or discouraged with these things. He needed a lot of support to keep trying. Lots of repetition and lots of recognition were essential strategies in working with Sam. We also reminded him often of how wonderful he felt when he accomplished something he had set out to do.

Sam was a master at avoiding things he didn't want to do. He stalled or he distracted you with conversation. It was easy for him to get off-task, especially when dealing with things that were difficult. He would start telling a story about something or just conversing; he loved doing that. Before you knew it, the time was up and Sam had not engaged in the activity. If I saw this happening with my aide or a volunteer, I would say, "Sam, you're telling Ms. Jones this wonderful story about la la la. Right now you're supposed to be (whatever the task was). She's going to help you finish (whatever the task was)." I would look at the adult and say, "Make sure you follow through." Then he or she would. This was the best way to get Sam to refocus and keep him on track in areas in which he did not excel.

Routines were important to Sam. If there was change in routine, he needed lots of advance notice that a change was coming. This was true at any transition time. It was hard for him to stop whatever it was he was doing, but he was like lots of other kids that way.

Emotional Development

Sam was a generally happy child; however, he had many fears. He often said he was afraid.

Sam was quite sensitive to sound. Loud noises upset him. Something like a fire drill (with the ringing buzzer) felt like the end of the world to him.

Anticipation played a big part in Sam's fears. He felt anxious a lot. He worried about what was going to happen and how to avoid anything he thought would be bad. Many times, when Sam said he was afraid, I found that explaining things or giving him a chance to be part of things, but with a definite exit strategy, helped him to cope. He often found out that he could manage the situation. That felt good to him.

Sam's parents and I agreed that we would work on his fears during the year. Here are some of the notes I wrote to keep them informed of how he was doing at school [*see Figure 7.4*]. This was also something I made sure to talk about at the IEP they had for him at the end of the year.

Figure 7.4. The teacher's notes to Sam's parents about his fears.

January 25	Sam cried during the story *Maia* (a chapter book about a dinosaur). He was afraid of bad things coming but stayed at group, sitting close to a parent who was visiting, and was okay.
January 26	Sam greeted me by saying he didn't want to hear Chapter 2 of *Maia*. We talked and I persuaded him to listen to part of it (he could bail out at any time). It really is a cool book. We also talked about lions and tigers—they're not mean, just hungry. After that, he stayed for the whole chapter.
January 27	We did the dinosaur dance in the gym. Sam thought he'd be afraid, but he wasn't. He had fun.
January 28	I read another "scary" book during large group today. Before I began reading, I talked about how funny it was going to be. Sam enjoyed it a lot. It was a good week!
February 24	Outside, Mike P. was growling at Sam. Sam was "scared" at first. When Mike and I reminded Sam that Mike was playing dinosaurs again, he stopped being afraid and played dinosaurs with Mike most of the morning.
March 3	Sam is a little afraid of Erik, a loud child in our class who is sometimes aggressive. Erik also intrigues him. Outside today we practiced saying loudly, "Stop it. I don't like that." Of course, after one successful use, Sam wanted to say it often—not always when called for. The whole group talked a little about thumbs up and thumbs down as another signal to help each other know when something was getting to be too intense or uncomfortable. We all agreed to try this. Sam said it was a good plan.
March 17	You mentioned that Sam is afraid of Erik's screaming. I liked your idea that he walk away when this happens or that he put his hands on his ears. I will follow up on those ideas here at school. Also, I noticed that sometimes Sam says that Erik is screaming when he really isn't. I am handling this by saying, "I'm listening for it. You listen, too. Do you hear him screaming?"

Designing Sam's Individual Education Plan

Before going to first grade, Sam was evaluated for special education services through his local school district. As his kindergarten teacher, I attended a meeting along with his mother, his speech therapist, his occupational therapist, a social worker, the school nurse, a psychologist, a special education teacher, and a general education teacher. We met together to discuss Sam's future education.

Following a discussion of what everyone knew about Sam, he was approved to receive special education services under the "other health impairments" category of the Individuals with Disabilities Education Act. We then developed his Individual Education Plan [see *Appendixes A and B*]. It was agreed that Sam would spend most of each day in a regular first-grade classroom. He would be assigned a paraprofessional aide to support his learning in the classroom. It was further determined that he would receive targeted programming for 1 hour per day in a resource room at his school. Finally, he would have speech therapy and occupational therapy throughout the year.

The day after Sam's IEP meeting, I was so gratified to receive this note from Sam's mother:

> Thank you so much for attending the IEP. Because of your advocacy, concern, and belief in Sam, the IEP was a nice experience for us. To be surrounded by people who see all that is good and possible in Sam was just wonderful. Thanks.

SAM'S MOTHER CONTINUES THE STORY

Sam in First Grade

Sam went to a new school for first grade. His resource room teacher was great. We had terrific two-way communication all year.

Things were different with the regular education teacher. We talked a little, but mostly she just said he was doing fine. At the beginning of the year, I offered to volunteer in Sam's classroom once a week. But the teacher said "no." It was my first public school experience. I didn't know that I had a right to go in there. Finally, at the end of the year, she allowed me to come in a few times. When I visited, I realized Sam's first-grade teacher had no real expectations for him. She never challenged him or corrected him. When the class would do certain activities, she made no effort to include him. She relied on the paraprofessional to do all the teaching to Sam. She never talked to the paraprofessional about lessons for him. He did learn some new things during the year, but it wasn't because of the classroom teacher.

During the year, Sam was really searching for someone to be his friend. Each time I met with the classroom teacher, I expressed my concern that he felt he wasn't making friends at school. One Saturday I called the resource room teacher, crying over something that just happened about this friend thing. She said, "Why don't you ask his teacher to put him in the friendship group?" They had a friendship group at the school for kids his age, but I didn't know about it. I had brought up the problem regarding friends over and over again at every single meeting, and that teacher never ever mentioned a group like that. I guess she didn't think he was capable of participating or that it would do any good.

He's going to a different classroom next year; maybe it will be better in second grade. I am planning on meeting with the teacher before school starts to get things going on the right track.

Epilogue

We don't know for sure about the future, which is good. A lot of people say, "What's going to happen?" We really don't know. I will just be so happy if he graduates from high school. If he goes to college, that would be the icing on the cake. My biggest hope is that he will get married. He is such a loving person and so affectionate. I think it would make him happy and he could make someone happy, too.

INFORMATION FOR EDUCATORS ABOUT THE "OTHER HEALTH IMPAIRMENTS" CATEGORY OF IDEA

Children who receive special education services under the "other health impairments" category of the Individuals with Disabilities Education Act (IDEA) vary greatly in their educational, social, emotional, and medical needs. Some children are born with the condition; others develop a health impairment during childhood (Turnbull, Turnbull, Shank, & Leal, 1999). In Sam's case, it is likely that his seizure disorder is a congenital condition; the complications that occurred from the bacterial meningitis are an acquired condition.

The three major criteria of the "other health impairments" category are limitations in strength, vitality, and alertness. Sam's seizure disorder affects his strength and vitality after he has a seizure. The seizure also affects his alertness to his environment. His poor muscle tone, frequent need to rest, difficulty with problem-solving skills, and other developmental delays are further signs of lack of vitality and alertness according to the IDEA.

Anyone might experience a seizure once in his or her life as the result of infection, low blood sugar, or injury. This does not mean that he or she has a seizure disorder (also referred to as epilepsy). However, about 1 in every 200 young children is at risk for multiple seizures throughout their lifetime. These youngsters, like Sam, are described as having a seizure disorder (Wolriach, 1984).

There are more than 150 underlying causes of epilepsy. Some of these include infections, lead poisoning, disturbances to the circulation of blood to the brain, high fevers, or brain injury. Yet in 70% of all cases, no definitive cause can be found (Epilepsy Foundation, 2000).

A seizure happens when there is an abnormal discharge of electrical energy in certain brain cells. When this occurs, a person may experience a brief period of unconsciousness or altered consciousness.

Seizures may be either generalized or partial in nature. Generalized seizures cause a loss of consciousness. There are two types of generalized seizures:

1. Tonic-clonic, or grand mal, seizures, which cause the child to fall and have a convulsion. One or more of the following symptoms often accompany a convulsion: falling, muscle spasms, drooling or "frothing" at the mouth, loss of bladder or bowel control, a temporary halt in breathing.
2. Absence seizures, which result in the child's losing consciousness for only a few seconds. The child and surrounding others may not even realize that a seizure has occurred. Absence seizures can happen as often as 100 times a day, resulting in severe impacts on learning (Epilepsy Foundation, 2000).

Partial seizures occur when the electrical discharge is limited to only one area of the brain. There are three types of partial seizures:

1. Temporal lobe or psychomotor seizures cause a dreamlike state (which the child does not remember later) in which the child makes random movements.
2. Focal sensory seizures cause the child to see or hear things that are not there.
3. Myoclonic seizures cause a child to look startled or in pain.

As with Sam, seizure disorders can often be controlled with medication. Even so, extreme stress, fatigue, and illness may still prompt a seizure. Thus it is important to remain alert to these factors and respond accordingly. In spite of all these precautions, a child may still experience a seizure while in your care. When this happens, you should know what to do, both for the child and for other children in the group:

- Your primary goal during a seizure is to keep the child's airway open. Blocked air passages may deprive the child's brain of oxygen, leading to brain damage.
- Your secondary goal is to keep a child from hurting himself or herself.
- Your third aim is to help all children in the group feel safe and secure.

Here is what to do if a child has a seizure in your early childhood setting:

- If the child is having trouble breathing, his or her airway may be blocked. Place the child facedown or on his or her side to allow secretions to drain and the tongue to come forward.
- If the child is not breathing, or if the child's lips start to turn blue, make sure the airway is clear and then give mouth-to-mouth resuscitation.
- If the child is breathing without difficulty, place him or her on the ground or floor in a safe area. Move all objects away from the child, and place cushions around his or her head if possible. Loosen tight clothing.
- Do not try to wedge the child's mouth open or place an object between the child's teeth, and do not attempt to restrain the child's movements.
- If breathing is normal and the seizure lasts just a few minutes, you can wait until it has subsided, reassure the child, then call the parent.
- Seek medical help if:
     A seizure lasts more than 5 minutes
     A second seizure follows the first
     An injury occurs during the seizure
     There is no previous history of seizures.
- Following a seizure, most children fall into a deep sleep. This is normal; allow the child to sleep.
- Do not attempt to give the child anything to eat or drink until he or she is awake and alert.
- When the child awakens, reassure the child that you are there and that he or she is safe. Help the child refresh him- or herself as appropriate (Epilepsy Foundation, 2000; Hingley, 1999).

HINTS FOR SUCCESS

Now that you have some information about how to help a child who is experiencing a seizure, here are some additional things you can do to support parents and the other children in your classroom.

1. Talk to the parents about their child and how they handle his or her seizures at home. Also discuss any environmental triggers that might prompt a seizure in the child (e.g., bright lights or certain odors).
2. Develop a seizure plan for your early childhood program. Assign tasks in advance to relevant adults in the program:
   Someone to stay with the child
   Someone to contact the parent
   Someone to remain with and talk to the other children
   Someone to call 911 (if necessary)
   Someone to accompany the child in the ambulance (if necessary)
3. Share your seizure plan with the parents. Make sure you are all comfortable with how a seizure will be handled if it occurs in your program.
4. Remain calm. This will reassure everyone that the child is safe and that the group is safe as well.
5. Keep accurate written records. Write down the length of the seizure, what the child was doing when the seizure took place, and what you did in response.
6. Answer children's questions matter-of-factly and honestly—"You're curious about what happened to Sam. Sometimes Sam's brain has too much energy. His body shows this energy. Once the energy is gone, he is tired and wants to rest" (Deiner, 1993).

QUESTIONS FOR DISCUSSION

1. What are some things you noticed about Sam that seem fairly typical for a child his age?
2. What factors contributed to Sam's inadequate first-grade experience? What roles could the first-grade teacher, the resource room teacher, and the principal have played differently to provide a higher-quality learning environment?
3. Sam's mother spoke about ways friends and family treated Sam and their family as a whole. Describe the ways in which you think you could be an adult friend or family member to someone like Sam and his family. List some things you would and would not do, using Sam's story to stimulate your thinking.
4. What lessons have you learned from Sam's story?

RESOURCES FOR EDUCATORS AND PARENTS

Epilepsy Foundation
4351 Garden City Drive

Landover, MD 20785
Phone: (800) 332-1000; (301) 459-3700
Website: http://www.apa.org/science/efa (retrieved 5/18/01)
This national nonprofit health organization is dedicated to the prevention and cure of seizure disorders, the alleviation of their effects, and the promotion of independence and an optimal quality of life for people with epilepsy.

The foundation catalogue offers a number of books, videos, pamphlets, and guides on epilepsy-related topics, such as:

- A video called Epilepsy: The Child and the Family
- A book entitled Does Your Child Have Epilepsy?
- Employment and legal information
- Information for teachers and recreational personnel

To order the catalogue or get answers to your questions on epilepsy, call the patient information service at the number given above.

REFERENCES

Deiner, P. L. (1993). *Resources for teaching children with diverse abilities*. New York: Harcourt Brace Jovanovich.

Epilepsy Foundation. (2000.) What to do if your child has a seizure. http://www.apa.org/science/efa (retrieved 5/18/01).

Hingley, A. (1999). Epilepsy: Taming the seizures and dispelling the myths. *FDA Consumer Magazine, 33* (1), 1–3.

Turnbull, A., Turnbull, R., Shank, M., & Leal, D. (1999). *Exceptional lives: Special education in today's schools*. Upper Saddle River, NJ: Merrill.

Wolriach, M. (1984). Seizure disorders. In J. Blackman (Ed.), *Medical aspects of developmental disabilities in children birth to three* (pp. 215–221). Rockville, MD: Aspen.

CHAPTER 8

Brian

"Just Bursting to Communicate"

It was after 5:00 P.M. The last child had gone home for the day. Kaeynti Johnson took a seat across from us. She looked tired. She had just finished a typically busy afternoon in her pre-primary special education classroom. "Let me tell you about Brian," she began. "He's such a neat little guy. These children are really great little kids inside. You just have to get to know who they are as people." With these words, her face lit up, and the fatigue seemed to melt away.

HIS TEACHER TELLS ABOUT BRIAN AND HERSELF

I have been teaching for 30 years. I started in special education for emotionally impaired children and began with first-graders. After several years, I moved to a teacher consultant position. I did not like that. I liked having my own classroom. I also began feeling that I was too far from where it all starts. Even first grade was too far from the beginning for these children. So I went back to graduate school in the pre-primary department. I also became involved with NAEYC [*the National Association for the Education of Young Children*]. I wanted to better understand those normal components of development we didn't get much of in special education. I learned a lot about typically developing kids, and I use that information every day along with my special education background. I have had a pre-primary special education class for the past 14 years, and I love it!

I have a mixed group of kids who have a variety of special needs. Every year it's different. I take the youngest that come into the program. They are 3.

There are 12 children in my class. I have an assistant and an aide. Children arrive by van. Learning begins the minute they walk in the door. Taking off their backpacks, greeting people, and putting on name tags are opportunities for learning. Our schedule looks a lot like a typical day in any preschool. In addition, we have an occupational therapist and a speech therapist that visit each week. They work in the classroom with the rest of the teachers and individually with children as needed. Many skills are addressed throughout the day—gross- and fine-motor skills, verbal skills, sensory-motor skills, visual-perceptual skills, appropriate academic skills, and social interaction.

I talk to the parents about its being a holistic program—that's the word I use. I say, "Yes, your child has a disability I need to deal with very deliberately, but my purpose is to educate your child as a whole person, too. When I need to think about the disability, I will. At the same time, I am going to treat him or her like I would any child, and that means focusing on all aspects of development." Most parents are pretty comfortable with that; they like that philosophy as long as they know there is special education expertise behind it. This year we have some children with severe disabilities in the program.

Brian's First Days at School

Brian entered my classroom as a 3-year-old, having been identified as needing special education for speech and language. There were also concerns about his behavior.

Brian had a bull-in-a-china-shop approach to the classroom. He did not look before he did anything. He did not think before he did anything. If somebody had a toy he wanted, he took it. He would pinch, down low, when he thought I wasn't looking. Or he would step on somebody's foot. He was pretty aggressive.

In the beginning, Brian lived inside himself. He played with trucks by himself. He played with blocks by himself. He didn't attempt to play with other children at all. If they had something he wanted, he took it, then left the area to play by himself.

When Brian started in my room, he could say a couple of sounds. *Ticka-ticka* was his favorite. That stood for just about everything. He would change the intonation a little for certain things, but that was the one sound he relied on. Many times, if you tried to get him to give you a different sound or a word, he would turn his head away, bury his face, or just shake his head, "no, no."

I observed him the first few days, and, of course, I had to intercede when negative things happened. But I immediately started to realize that the aggression was a result of his inability to communicate. His actions were saying, "I have no way to communicate with you. Not only do I have no way to communicate with you, but also I have no control over anything in my life. If I can't communicate, I can't control anything."

Understanding Brian's Communication Disorder

Brian's official diagnosis was apraxia. This meant it was difficult for him to produce language. Because of brain damage or lack of development, he had to do a tremendous amount of conscious processing (both mental and physical) to make sounds that come naturally to most children.

In addition, Brian had had serious recurrent ear infections that caused intermittent hearing loss. Although he wasn't diagnosed as having a permanent hearing loss or hearing impairment at the time he was in my class, there is no question that hearing was a real issue. They had tried putting tubes in his ears to increase his hearing abilities, but that didn't seem to help much. The first time I met her, Brian's mom said, "I don't think he hears me." I came to the same conclusion. I think he didn't listen to people, even when he could hear (physically), because words didn't have a lot of meaning for him. If you can hear some of the time, but you can't hear most of time, you can't rely on words for meaning, so why bother listening?

Besides coming to preschool Monday through Friday, Brian had two 30-minute sessions with the speech therapist weekly.

Goals for Brian

One goal I had in working with Brian was to help him become less aggressive. A second was to enhance his communication skills. These two goals were complementary. Here are the strategies I used to work towards them.

Strategy 1: Intervening When Brian Was Aggressive

Whenever Brian would hurt someone, I would intercede. I would take his hand, draw him close to the other little boy or girl, and say, "Look, look what you did! See her face. She's crying. Look at her face; she's crying. You hurt her. Did you want to tell her something?" Next, I gave him the words that I thought he wanted to say (e.g., Say, "I want it." Say, "want." Say, "Can I have it later?"). To do this, I had to be a pretty good observer. Sometimes he would try to pull away. He really didn't want to do this at first. However, as time went on, I noticed he did want to communicate. He kept getting closer and closer to me. He would squeeze up against me during these little conversations to try to hear words, to try to find out what was being said. I made sure to repeat the same few words over and over again.

We have a spot in the classroom that we call the thinking spot. If children need some time away from their peers, we have them sit in the thinking spot for a while. That really works well for some children. However, I didn't see the thinking spot as the best strategy for Brian—time away from the group wouldn't quell his frustration. The main problem was communication. So that's what we worked on.

I don't think Brian really understood that he was hurting people in the beginning. He was just going after what he wanted. Once he understood he was hurting someone, it was easier for him to stop. Hurting people was not what he wanted to do.

Brian's aggressive behavior didn't stop immediately. His behavior change was gradual. It took a year for the aggression to pretty much disappear. However, it was only about 2 months before it got to be tolerable. Around November, my aide and I looked at each other and realized we were not having so many confrontations with Brian anymore.

While we were working through this aggression thing, Brian's parents and I talked about medication. I just didn't think that was the route to go for at least a year. I wanted to observe him much more before we got into that. I'm very glad we didn't go with medication to start. It turned out to be unnecessary.

Strategy 2: Establishing Expectations for Brian's Behavior

It was important to me that Brian feel part of the group. This included following some basic classroom rules expected of all the children. Sitting at group time was one of these rules. Early in the year, Brian decided that he absolutely wasn't going to sit with the others at group time. In the beginning I did allow him a bit more leeway because I knew he didn't quite understand what was going on. However, once he had some experience with group time, and he still wouldn't comply, I assisted him. I helped him sit down, and I said, "This is group time; you have to be here in group time for a few minutes." Our group time is very short, so it was not a big trauma. To help him comply, I would have him sit next to me or next to my aide. Many times I had him sit on my lap, and she (the aide) would lead the group. As he became better able to sit through the activities, I tried to have him stay there on his own. Each child in my class has a carpet square to designate his or her place to sit or lean. I would help him sit down on his carpet square and say, "This is your space, or would you like this one? You can have this one. I'll help you sit here."

Sometimes Brian sat and sometimes he didn't. Sometimes we would have to repeat the expectation three or four times. Each time he got up, my aide or I would retrieve him. We were very consistent. We knew if we stayed calm and persistent, the day would come when he would sit in group without our help. Eventually, children always do. Some children take a long, long time. We had to follow through with our expectations many times a day. Besides setting a limit, we made sure group time was fun, too. By midyear, Brian was more successful and found that group time could be an enjoyable part of the day.

Strategy 3: Compensating for Brian's Poor Hearing and Listening Skills

Most important, I would try to make sure Brian was looking at me when I spoke. I often moved toward him as I was speaking. I spoke slowly and distinctly. Short sentences were best. I would repeat the same words often. I also kept up a running commentary about things in the classroom. If Brian were building with blocks, I would say things like, "You have a blue block. Now you put a red block on top." Children learn to listen more carefully by hearing words used in relation to their day-to-day activities.

Strategy 4: Introducing Sign Language

We decided to try sign language with Brian. We picked certain words (such as *thank you, more, wait, want*) and repeated them often, combining the word and the sign [*see Figure 8.1*]. I would say to Brian, "You can tell Lawrence something. You can say *thank you*." I would then sign *thank you* and show him what to do.

At first Brian didn't respond. So I would go behind him and say, "Don't forget to tell him *thank you*." Then I would take his hand and literally help him sign the words. Of course, he started out fighting the whole process. When that happened, as soon as we made the sign together, no matter how much he struggled, I would say, "Oh what a great job, you said *thank you*." We did a lot of that. I'd say, "Tell me *more* if that's what you want. Tell me *more*." He would put his hands in his lap. In that case, I would take his hands, mine over his, and hold them together to make the sign for *more*. As soon as his hands came together, I would

Figure 8.1. Examples of signs Ms. Johnson used to communicate with Brian.

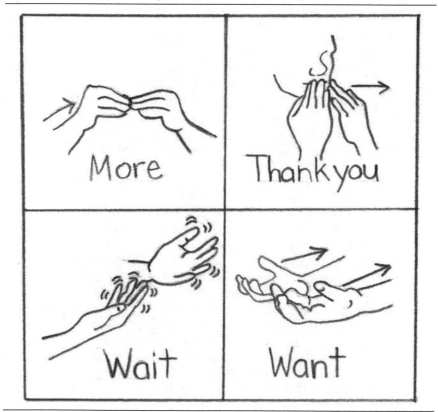

say, "Oh, you want more. Okay." And I would give him more. These little coaching sessions were clues to him that he could communicate.

Once he realized there were signs for things, we were signing all over the room. He was like a sponge. His actions clearly said, "I want to do this; I want more tools to communicate with you." Learning a few simple signs opened Brian's world. When he realized he had the power to communicate his needs and wants, things started to turn around immediately.

Sign language was never a substitute for speaking. Instead, it served as a bridge or scaffold from silence to more intelligible speech and language.

Strategy 5: Combining Signs and Sounds

Once he mastered some basic signs, I told Brian he had to give me a sound with each one. So if he signed *thank you*, I would say, "What? I couldn't hear you. Tell me *thank you*." So he would say *ticka-ticka* and sign *thank you*.

In another situation I might say, "What do you want? Tell me what you want." Since he couldn't really tell me what he wanted, I would give him two choices. "Do you want the barn, or do you want the trucks?" Then he could point to the thing he wanted and make a sound. Again, it was empowering. He got the message—"You're going to help me to communicate. And I *can* communicate in ways you'll understand."

Strategy 6: Combining Strategies at Home and School

Brian's mom said she was really struggling with his aggressive behavior at home. We talked about giving him choices at home just like we were doing at school. His mom and I developed a picture system to make this easier. For instance, on the refrigerator there was a picture of juice, a picture of milk, and a picture of water. He had to touch the picture and give her a sound. *Ticka-ticka* was all right in the beginning. He just had to produce some kind of sound to get what he wanted. If he didn't make a sound, he didn't get whatever it was he wanted. We used picture symbols at school, too. Many were the same ones he used at home.

There were times (at home and at school) when he was furious at having to do this. He was furious—but he was also excited because he was ready to communicate. He was just bursting to communicate. He would take you to things. He would point to things. He wanted a way—he needed a way to get out and talk to you.

Strategy 7: Using Different Sounds to Represent Different Words

We gradually moved to expecting Brian to make different sounds for different things. We started with *M* and *B*. For instance, if Brian wanted milk and said *ticka-ticka*, I would say, "You can come closer than that. Try this, *mmmmilk*." Whenever I made the *M* sound, I would lightly touch the skin above his upper lip and draw my finger from left to right. This is called a touch-cue strategy.

He wasn't sure at first that he liked that idea of making different sounds. But when he realized that it was going to give him more power to communicate, he just switched over. *Ticka-ticka* became less prominent, and he began to make some new sounds.

Strategy 8: Helping Brian Feel Successful

Anytime Brian did what I asked him to do, I made sure to help him recognize that he had been successful. I would make a little face, put my thumbs up, or say, "Good job." I wanted him to get the message "You're doing okay," or "You're on the right track." Sometimes, I just wanted him to know that I saw him and noticed that he was doing okay—not because he had accomplished anything in particular, but just because it was fun to have him around. There was a lot of that with him.

Reading Brian's Cues

In the beginning, I had to be a pretty good observer because Brian gave mixed messages. For instance, he would sometimes act like he didn't want me to pay attention to him. He would pull away or look away, but then he would watch me out of the corner of his eye to see if I was still looking. Sometimes he would run and do exactly the opposite of what I told him to do. The whole time this was happening, he would be looking over his shoulder to make sure I was watching.

At first, he wouldn't sit on my lap. He wouldn't cuddle. I had to be open to that. I would sit on the floor with him, and we would play with trucks or we would play with the farm animals. I let him decide how close he wanted to be. Over time, when we played, he got closer and closer to me. Eventually, it got to the point that if I sat down, he was right on my lap.

Before he learned to sign, Brian would take my hand and put it on something. Then he would look at me and he would say *ticka-ticka*. That might mean "What is this?" or "Can I play with this?" or "Is it time to play with this?" He might take me to an area of the room, and I would have to play a guessing game about what he wanted. Sometimes I figured things out because of his body language or based on a certain look in his eyes.

Once Brian felt comfortable with me, I began to make some deliberate mistakes interpreting his gestures. He would point to something, and I would act like I didn't understand right away or I would make the wrong guess. Before he became too frustrated, I gave him what I thought he wanted. In this way, I began creating a need for him to use speech to be more readily understood. I had to watch closely, so as not to move beyond his tolerance for frustration. I wanted him to be a slightly disconcerted by my "stupidity," but not so much so that he gave up or became really distraught.

At group time I learned never to call on him first. The first few times I did, it was a dreadful mistake. He either shut down or he left. A couple of times, he kicked someone—not at that very moment, but soon thereafter. I came to recognize that it was better to call on him third or fourth and sometimes not at all. I would let him call that shot. I would have to watch carefully to see how he might react. To make things easier for him, I would call on at least two children first; before I called on the third, I would tell him he'd be next (e.g., "Allison is going now; you'll be next."). That kind of warning gave him some processing time before it was his turn. This strategy worked really well.

If we were going to do sharing time at group and he brought something in, I would make sure we rehearsed a little during our free-choice period (which occurred before group time). I would go through his backpack and say, "Oh, you brought a yellow Big Bird. Look. What did you bring? You brought a yellow Big Bird. " And I would describe what he brought four or five times. "Are you going to show yellow Big Bird at group time? You could come and stand by me and we could do it together." In this way, we rehearsed what was going to happen. Sometimes it worked; sometimes it didn't. I mean, he might show his sharing item, or he might not.

Establishing a Relationship with Brian's Family

Brian's mom came with him to our open house the first day. She was very apologetic because he was very aggressive and wouldn't listen to her. She begged him to behave. It didn't do any good. She was so embarrassed. That day, I told her that Brian was not the first child I had ever seen who behaved that way. I said to her, "He's going to be okay. In 3 months you're not going to believe what we'll be able to accomplish. We will just have to work together. We are going to become really close, you and I." She looked relieved but anxious when she left.

Brian's mom and I talked on the telephone quite a bit the first month. I also had a chance to speak with his father. I think you have to develop rapport with parents, and that takes time. Mom and Dad both came to some classroom events (two conferences, a holiday party, and a field trip). I also asked them to visit the classroom a few times.

It was hard for them to see Brian in school. They were embarrassed by his behavior, but we talked a lot about what they would see when they visited. The same things I did with Brian, I did with his mom and dad. I would say things like, "This is what you're going to see. Let's walk through what we are going to do. Let's talk about how we are going to respond." We talked a great deal about what their responses needed to be at home, both in terms of Brian's aggressive behavior and in terms of his language needs. I tried to explain how I was interpreting what Brian was really trying to communicate. It is a bit more tolerable to cope with your child's negative behavior if you understand that he *can't* do some things, rather than thinking he simply *won't* do them. That seemed to help. We did become pretty close; his mom called me quite a bit. We would talk about behavior. We talked about what was going on at school and in their household.

At the end of the year, his dad took me aside and said, "We don't know what we would ever have done without this program. We were getting desperate. He's a different child today from what he was in August. We are so happy. He is just a different little boy." That felt pretty good.

Advice for Early Childhood Professionals

Based on my experience, I can suggest some additional strategies for working with young children like Brian.

1. *Don't take young children's aggressive behavior personally.* Rarely do 3– and 4–year-old children intend to hurt you deliberately. I've been bitten; I've been pinched; children for various reasons have hit me. I do not for 1 minute think there was any real maliciousness directed towards me as an individual. I just happened to be the adult who got in the way.
2. *Start with a fresh outlook every day.* There will be rough days working with young children. Try to come into the classroom not having forgotten yesterday but not anticipating the worst either. Children like Brian are very sensitive to adult moods. If you are anxious, they will

know something's wrong. However, they won't interpret your anxiety accurately. They will simply think you don't like them.

3. *Prepare yourself to teach.* Watch each child at play. Think about your goals for the children. Plan ways to achieve those goals. Approach children's language needs and behavioral needs the same way you would approach goals related to reading. Be prepared, have the materials you need on hand, and think through what you are going to do in advance. Develop specific strategies to match your goals; then adapt them to fit the children's responses. That's how you can individualize your teaching to meet the needs of each child.

4. *Enjoy the children for who they are.* Like them. If you like them, you can accomplish a lot. Look for the things that are neat about these kids. Don't just focus on their problems. If I didn't like the children, I couldn't do this job. I genuinely enjoy being with them. I love my job, and I really like the kids. And laugh! Children love it when adults laugh. Kids will respond so much better if they get a sense that you think it's fun to be with them.

5. *Anticipate frustrating situations and offer encouragement before asking children to engage in challenging tasks.* Let's say you're doing a spelling activity, and you know a child is stressed at spelling time. Before you begin the task, tell her, "I know this is going to be tough, but I know you can do it. I'll go slow." Use words and actions that say, "I'll do what you need to make this a reachable goal. I'm going to be here. I'm going to be your support person." This is the kind of thing a child with special needs benefits from hearing ahead of time.

6. *Convey your acceptance of the child, especially when things go poorly.* If a child like Brian temporarily loses control or does something else that's really horrible in your mind or in his, you must communicate that you don't dislike him as a result. It is essential for him to understand that you still think he is an okay person. You like him and that's not going to stop, even as you work with him to change negative behaviors. Relationships are important to children like Brian. The child has to know that he is still okay in your eyes. If he develops the idea that you dislike him, he will do everything to fit that negative image and you will have problems.

7. *Keep your expectations high.* I was told by a couple of people that Brian's apraxia was going to make it impossible for him to create any new sounds. They said I should just teach him to sign and forget the rest. I said, "Oh, we'll see." I had to be realistic, but I kept expecting that he could eventually speak. Don't lower your standards too quickly. Don't assume the child can't do things because those things are diffi-

cult. You aren't doing a child any favors by treating her as though she can't learn.

8. *Analyze situations to figure out what went right and what went wrong.* Avoid simply pressing on without reflecting on your teaching. Think about lessons that go well; analyze the ones that fall apart, too. If you are in a situation with a child like Brian and it all falls apart (I've had hundreds of those), say, "Okay, why did this fall apart? What happened here?" Assume, "It's not Brian's fault; it's not my fault. What happened?" Think to yourself, "I'm going to look at this as a learning experience," not, "Oh my gosh, what a horrible morning we had." Instead, think, "Okay, we don't want to do this again. How do we avoid it? Okay, that's one that I have to let go; I have to let that day go."

9. *Go back to strategies that didn't work earlier; try them again later in the year.* As you reflect, don't throw the baby out with the bath water. If you have a technique you want to try and it doesn't work the first time, don't say, "Oh, I'll never do that again!" Sometimes you have to try a technique four, five, or six times. You may have to keep it for later. You may have used it too soon. You need not necessarily abandon a particular technique forever; you may simply have to save it for later in the year.

Hopes for Brian's Future

Brian was so unhappy when he first started school. During that first year in my room, I saw some glimmers of him thinking, "I'm beginning to like my life. I am comfortable with who I am." My hope is that those feelings will continue to blossom.

I'd like to see Brian be a functioning person in society. He doesn't have to have great achievements, but the happiness piece is really important to me. I hope he has a happy life.

Epilogue

Brian is now in a class for 4–year-olds with special needs. It is likely that he will stay in pre-primary special education for at least 1 more year after this. Then he will go into a regular education program for kindergarten. I am sure he will continue to have speech and language services in elementary school.

Brian's language is still impaired. If you were to talk to him, you would find him very difficult to understand. So progress is relative. It's really relative. Brian continues to struggle with new words. He struggles a lot. However, he has the biggest desire to communicate that I have ever seen.

I talked to Brian's current teacher a few days ago. It is beginning to look like he will grow out of the ear infections. If that happens, his hearing will become more stable. With any luck, he will experience only minimal hearing loss at levels that won't include speech. His teacher said his conduct is great and that things are moving right along. I was thrilled!

INFORMATION FOR EDUCATORS ABOUT APRAXIA

Apraxia is just one of several communication disorders young children may experience. Depending on the definitions used, children with communication disorders (including listening, speaking, writing, and reading) make up about 5% to 10% of the U.S. population from birth to age 8. In general, children's communication is impaired when

> there are deviations in the formation, expression or understanding of language. Characteristics of impaired communication include poor concepts, inability to follow directions, speechlessness, speech confusion, and poor comprehension. A child's speech is impaired when it deviates so much from the speech of other children that it calls attention to itself, interferes with communication, or causes the child to be self-conscious. (Deiner, 1993, p. 138)

Because language is so closely related to all aspects of development, children who manifest communication disorders often have difficulties and/or delays in other arenas, such as in developing problem-solving strategies or social skills.

Children with apraxia have great difficulty positioning their face, tongue, lips, and jaw to produce speech sounds or to sequence those sounds into syllables and words. Apraxia occurs when the area of the brain that tells the muscles how to move and what to do to make a particular sound or series of sounds is damaged or not fully developed. Even when children know what they want to say, they cannot say it correctly at that particular time. Sometimes they cannot even begin. Either the wrong sound comes out or many sounds are left out all together. Because these errors are not under children's voluntary control, they often cannot correct them, even when trying their hardest (Guild, 2000).

Children with apraxia have few speech sounds they can use automatically. Consequently, as demonstrated in Brian's case, children often rely on a simple syllable, such as *ticka-ticka*, to stand for almost everything. Once a child reaches the point where he or she can use several different consonant sounds, the main characteristic of apraxia is inconsistency. For instance, Brian may be able to say *M* at the beginning of a word as long as it is followed by *I*, such as in the word *milk*. However, he may have difficulty saying *M* when it is followed by *O*, as in *mop*. Sorting out these various combinations and using them at the appropriate time requires deliberate effort and much work. Here are some characteristics of apraxia as children emerge beyond the single-sound phase:

• Children may say single words but have difficulty stringing words together.
• Children may repeat words other people say but have difficulty generating new words without an immediate model to imitate.
• Children lose words. Certain words a child can say one day may be difficult to retrieve another day.
• Children find it difficult to put words in the correct sequence and later remember what the sequence should be.
• Children have difficulty learning to read and write in ways that mirror the challenges they experience with oral language.

Childhood apraxia is not something children grow out of. However, with proper intervention early in life, many children with this disorder learn to speak more clearly and to communicate effectively (Portwood, 1999). Such intervention includes intensive speech therapy coupled with many "typical" speech experiences in a supportive environment at home and at school.

HINTS FOR SUCCESS

Besides the strategies outlined by Ms. Johnson, here are more ideas for working with children like Brian in the early childhood setting.

1. Create a warm environment in which routines are predictable and well structured.
2. Accept whatever children say at first. Praise them for trying. If a child says something incorrectly, avoid saying, "No." Instead, say, "That's right," then restate the child's message using correct sounds/words.
3. If you understand what a child has said, repeat the words so he or she knows you understood. This not only reinforces speech and language, it also provides a model for the child to hear and imitate the next time.
4. Support the child's speech therapy by following through with speech drills the speech therapist might ask you to carry out in the classroom. Carry these out for a few minutes each day at a specified time during

the session. Avoid random practice sessions. Consistency helps children like Brian learn to anticipate what will be happening and gives them a chance to process what might be expected.

5. Use picture boards, sign language, and other physical aids to support children's efforts to communicate while simultaneously working on oral language skills.

6. Interact with children as they play. Follow the child's lead. Imitate what the child does, describe the child's activities, and avoid asking direct questions.

7. Pause long enough to allow the child to communicate. Do not rush children or finish their thoughts for them if they are trying to make a sound.

8. Rather than suggesting solutions to children, ask open-ended questions about next steps that they can show you as well as refer to verbally (e.g., "You are building a long bridge. Where will it go next?").

9. Reinforce approximations of desired behavior. Provide encouragement, while also challenging the child to try things just slightly beyond his or her reach.

10. Some children resort to physical solutions when placed in situations that are too demanding of them cognitively or linguistically. Assess situations to see if the child's physical reactions (e.g., running away, turning away, lashing out) are indications that the task is too demanding and needs to be simplified. Adapt accordingly.

QUESTIONS FOR DISCUSSION

1. What stood out to you about Brian's story?
2. What evidence did you see of the mother's willingness to partner with the teacher?
3. Think of a simple activity you might carry out with children in your classroom. How would you have to adapt that activity to accommodate Brian?
4. How do you think this teacher felt at the end of the day? How were her feelings about her professional role similar to or different from those of the other teachers you have read about in this book?
5. Consider Brian coming into your kindergarten class in 2 years. How would you prepare yourself to meet his needs in a setting with 21 other more typically developing children? How could other children be engaged in supporting Brian's language development? How could you mange his aggressive behavior if it reappeared when you have almost twice as many chldren as this teacher had in her classroom?

RESOURCES FOR EDUCATORS AND PARENTS

Books and CDs

Hamaguchi, P. M. (1995). *Childhood speech, language, and listening problems: What every parent should know.* New York: Wiley.

Portwood, M. (1999). *Developmental dyspraxia—Identification and intervention: A manual for parents and professionals* (2nd ed.). New York: Fulton.

Schwartz, S., & Miller, J. E. H. (1996). *The new language of toys: Teaching communication skills to children with special needs* (a guide for parents and teachers). New York: Woodbine House.

Wheeler, C. (1997). *Simple signs.* New York: Puffin.

Wheeler, C. (1997). *More simple signs.* New York: Puffin.

Lande, A., Wiz, B., & Morris, S. E. (Abridged edition, 2000). *Marvelous mouth music for speech therapy and beyond.* Belle Curve Records.

CD for children ages 4–8.

Available Online

Childhood Apraxia of Speech Association of North America
http://www.apraxia.org
Sharon Gretz, whose son has childhood apraxia of speech, founded the CASANA in 1997. The organization's Website is designed to provide accessible and understandable information regarding childhood apraxia of speech to parents and professionals.

Developmental Apraxia of Speech
http://www.tayloredmktg.com/dyspraxia/das.html
This Website presents an excellent article by Ann S. Guild, MACCC/SLP, with some additions by Tracy Vail, MSCCC/SLP, and is reproduced with their permission in order to help families, special educators, and speech language pathologists understand apraxia of speech.

REFERENCES

Deiner, P. L. (1993). *Resources for teaching children with diverse abilities* (2nd ed.). New York: Harcourt Brace Jovanovich.

Guild, A. S. (2000). *Developmental verbal apraxia.*
http://tayloredmktg.com/dyspraxia/das.html (retrieved 6/5/01).

Portwood, M. (1999). *Developmental dyspraxia—Identification and intervention: A manual for parents and professionals* (2nd ed.). New York: Fulton.

C H A P T E R   9

Daniel

Supported by a Team

Kristie Meyers is a teacher for the toddler class at a private, tuition-based preschool. Children in her class range from 2 to 3 years old. Her program provides time before the year begins in August to visit every child in his or her home. She admitted she was a bit embarrassed to describe how she first met and started to get to know Daniel.

HIS TEACHER TELLS DANIEL'S STORY

I met Daniel in August at his home visit, just before the schoolyear started. He had blond hair, big blue eyes, and a chubby round face. At first I felt a little uncomfortable because, for some reason, I hadn't been told in advance that Daniel has Down syndrome. I walked in, and his mom assumed that I knew.

When I started to play with Daniel, I quickly learned that his communication ability at that time was one-word utterances, and I couldn't understand him much. His mom acknowledged that Daniel, who was 3 years old, has Down syndrome and was just learning to talk. I knew that would be a challenge. Then his mom said, "Miss Meyers, you also know that Daniel has juvenile diabetes, right?" And I said, smiling as best I could, "No, that will be new for me as well." At that point his mom was quite concerned. Daniel had never been left with a caregiver other than at a church nursery school on Sunday morning; rarely was he away from his mother's side. I knew I would be dealing with parental separation as well as the usual child-separation issues. She wanted to know if I would agree to learn to test Daniel's blood, learn about the signs indicating when his blood-sugar level was getting low, and do shots at school. I thought, Oh my gosh! That first meeting with Daniel was a little shocking.

Getting to Know Daniel's Physical Abilities and Limitations

I have come to realize that just because a child has Down syndrome, I can't make the assumption that the child is just like another child I worked with before. There might be some similarities, but there are always differences. Children are all individuals. Daniel not only had juvenile diabetes and Down syndrome, but numerous things had gone wrong at his delivery. As a result, he had had multiple surgeries. I mean, he had gone through a lot.

When he started preschool, Daniel was 3 years, 3 months old. He had been walking for only 2 months on his own without assistance. Up to that time he had always been carried or assisted with a walker. When he started to walk, he'd go a few feet and then he would just sit down. He'd put his arms up as if to say, "Carry me." Daniel tired quite easily, and he napped in the afternoon. Daniel also walked very slowly and had difficulty climbing stairs.

In addition, Daniel didn't really enjoy anything that required coordination of his fingers. Because his physical development was delayed, he had small hands and fingers. His fine-motor skills weren't developed. He had a really hard time wrapping his fingers around crayons, markers, paintbrushes, and the like. I hadn't ever dealt with a child who was so far behind in terms of fine-motor skills. As the year got started, I talked with his occupational therapist, who came to the classroom once a week to observe and work with him on strengthening and coordinating the muscles in his hands and fingers. I wanted to find out what we could be doing differently for Daniel in the fine-motor area. It was exciting when she told me all the things we were providing already (modeling dough, beads, sand, water play, finger painting) were exactly what he needed. However, she noticed Daniel wasn't choosing to engage in those kinds of activities, and he really needed the practice. She recommended that we actively invite Daniel into fine-motor activities. That was very helpful.

In the beginning, my instructional aide, my student teacher, and I underestimated Daniel's gross-motor abilities. We recognized that one of Daniel's initial fears was that other children would bump into him. Even though he had lots of physical experiences with his two big brothers, they were careful with him. But here at school there were more children at his eye level, so there was an adjustment period for him as far as being around little children, especially on the playground with another class. For example, it took him a while before he would go on the tire swing with anybody else. We allowed him time to watch and try it alone. When he was on the equipment, we made sure we spotted him for safety by standing very close to him. I thought he was liable to fall backwards. One day Daniel's physical therapist came to talk to me during our outdoors time. It was the second week of school. Daniel was on the climber; I could see from a distance that he was going down the slide by himself. I think his physical capabilities were higher than anyone had anticipated. It was really exciting to see him just smile, climb up the climber, and go down that slide. All the teachers watched him do it; we stood there with looks of shock on our faces. His desire to take risks was amazing. Also, his abilities were higher than we knew.

As the year went on, Daniel gradually tried more gross-motor activities. I remember at the beginning of the year he wouldn't even look at the scooter, a flat 12–inch plastic square with rotating wheels on each corner that children use to scoot around on the gym floor while kneeling, sitting, or in a prone position. Weeks later, he would sit on it if we would push him. Pretty soon he started choosing the scooter without coaxing. The day he moved the scooter without help was a huge deal for us, because we were working on developing his leg muscles. My student teacher took a picture of Daniel as he pushed the scooter by himself. We rejoiced over this accomplishment.

Learning About Juvenile Diabetes

When Daniel's mom realized I didn't know about juvenile diabetes, she showed me, right there at the home visit, how to test his blood. I thought, "Oh, this is really going to be hard." But watching Daniel hold his finger out very matter-of-factly, and at his young age, I was very impressed.

Interacting with Daniel meant building a trusting relationship in which he would allow me to test his blood, keep him safe at school, and make sure that he always had what he needed to stabilize his physical condition. That meant having a ready source of sugar available for him (orange juice in the refrigerator) at all times. I also had to educate myself and the staff about the disease. I arranged for a diabetes education coordinator from the local hospital to come and give a workshop for me and my staff, to teach us about juvenile diabetes. To test Daniel's blood, she explained, he would bring a glucose kit to school everyday. It contained a small box that had a special little stick stuck into the top. We would fill that with a tiny bit of Daniel's blood. To get the blood, we'd use a needle that was in a plastic encasement, so it was never touched by anyone. We'd do a little twist and a poke on Daniel's finger. Then we had to massage his finger until blood came to the top and filled the stick. That gave us a number on the machine that told us his glucose level at the time. There were a range of levels that were good and a range that were not good. If his number was much lower than acceptable, we knew we had to get some orange juice into him right away. If the reading was much higher, that meant we shouldn't allow him any sugar. She also taught us to look for physical indications that his blood sugar was getting low, such as when his skin color looked more white, when his eyes were red, or when he appeared more irritable. Sometimes irritability was really difficult to judge. Daniel got irritable at times, as is typical for any 3-year-old. We'd be guessing it was just typical behavior, but most often we found it was low blood sugar.

Teaching Others About Daniel's Needs

Daniel's mom came into the classroom one day early in the year and actually tested him in front of the other children. We wanted them to get comfortable with the procedure. That's also why we made a children's book with pictures about Daniel's testing and put it in the book corner. We also talked about it with the children in the simplest terms, explaining what glucose is.

I trained my support staff and student teacher to test Daniel's blood. I wanted to be sure that all the adults were able to do it. If I wasn't there on a particular day, I had to be sure Daniel's needs would be met. I had each adult demonstrate that she could do a blood test. Daniel got so used to this routine that when we'd say, "Show me a finger, Daniel," he would just keep doing what he was doing, stick out a finger, and some-times not even look that way.

When I met with Daniel's specialist team at his meeting [*see Appendix A*], the first thing the school district representative asked was, "Miss Meyers, you're willing to do the blood test at school?" I told the group, "Yes, I see that as necessary to care for Daniel's physical needs while he's at school, and as his teacher that's a big part of my job. I also stay certified for first aid and CPR, and I make myself accessible to his mom by phone." They seemed rather surprised.

I think all early childhood programs are going to have to learn to deal with juvenile diabetes because there are more and more kids like Daniel being diagnosed. Recently I was on the Internet and communi-cated with the director of a full-day program that is caring for a child with juvenile diabetes. She needed help and was reaching out through the NAEYC [*National Association for the Education of Young Children*] Website. She really didn't know what to do; they were having the dad come from work on his breaks to test the child's blood. That wasn't making the director feel very comfortable, because no one on staff knew what to do in an emergency. I sent her everything I was doing, and she thanked me. This is an area where more education of early childhood profes-sionals is needed.

Daniel's Family

Daniel's mom is by profession a speech therapist. She has lots of skills for helping him use language. In the beginning, she stayed available everyday, practically living in our parent lounge for the first 2 months of school. I think she was really concerned that if he went "low" [*if his blood-sugar level dropped*], there would be things we couldn't handle. Eventu-ally, when she was comfortable enough to leave the building, she gave us her cell phone number so we could call her. I think she needed to have continuous reassurance that the school would deal with all of Daniel's challenges. I asked her lots of questions and also had my stu-dent teacher call her from time to time. If there was a question, I wanted Daniel's mom to feel that all of us were aware and knew how to handle his issues.

His parents were wonderful advocates for Daniel. They were so involved with him, not making him different from the rest of the family, protecting him in a certain way, but being okay with who he was. I learned Daniel had two older brothers in school and a dad who worked full time. Daniel's family ties were very strong. I saw his dad and his brothers on a couple of occasions when they all came to our family portfolio celebrations twice a year to view Daniel's collection of his work, anecdotal records about how he interacted in the classroom, and photographs of him working and playing with other children. Daniel's family also attended the end-of-the-year picnic. Daniel went to church with his family and to all of his brothers' sporting events. His world was very big because he interacted with lots of people. Daniel's special condition was handled very openly. For his "All About Me" book, they sent in pictures of the whole family in the intensive care unit holding Daniel when he was an infant. They involved their two older children right from the beginning. They all got to know who this little person was and what kind of challenges he was going to have, but also how wonderful a gift he was; the family really embraced this child. The brothers teased him just as they would any other brother. They seemed to enjoy having Daniel in their lives.

Daniel's Special Support Team

I gradually came to know all of the players on Daniel's support team [see Figure 9.1]. Daniel had been having speech therapy for some time and was also being seen regularly by an occupational therapist, a physical therapist, the family physician, and a diabetes specialist. Another important member of his team was the early-on coordinator, who was provided by the school district where Daniel will eventually go to elementary school. She coordinated all the services provided Daniel from birth through age 3. When he reached 3 years of age, the family requested that she continue him on her caseload, and the district agreed.

The family doctor had an ongoing struggle attempting to monitor and adjust the amount of insulin Daniel was getting and how often he got it. Often Daniel and his mom visited the doctor early in the morning, and then came to school late. He would be more tired when he got an insulin injection. This in turn affected his physical abilities.

In our state special education services are provided through the school district where the child lives and where the child will eventually attend school. The school district where Daniel lived wanted him to go to a PPI [pre-primary impaired] program in that town; that's what they offer to children like Daniel. But his mom was not inclined to start PPI yet, for he had just started school in our program. She was worried that having him attend PPI in addition to our class would be too long a day for him. Our preschool is located in a different school district. Because Daniel spent more of his day here, this local school district also got involved in providing services and in helping to formulate his education plan. At the IEP meeting, there was a discussion about which district would

Figure 9.1. Daniel's support team.

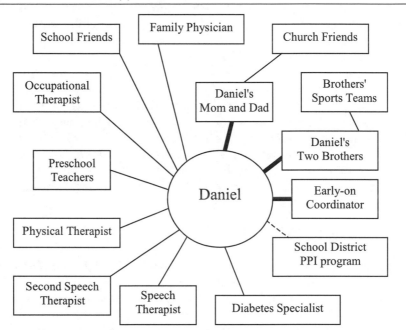

provide the speech therapy and his other needs. It was finally determined that two speech therapists would work with Daniel, one in his hometown and one here at our school. His physical therapist, occupational therapist, and early-on coordinator would all come here to work with him. Every specialist who came into my classroom left written reports, and usually I talked to them about what they were seeing. Normally this happened during the regular preschool day. But if there wasn't enough time, I met with them on my planning morning.

Teaching Daniel Language

One of the larger challenges Daniel faced was communication. From the beginning he was very social; he smiled and rarely cried. When he wanted something, he would give a look or make a sound. He had ways of communicating his needs very early. However, his use of words was very limited. At first, he might say "ju." We would ask, "Daniel, do you want juice?", and he would say "no" or "yuh" in some way. As the schoolyear went on, he could tell us better what his needs were.

Daniel was receiving speech therapy for 1 hour a week at another building. His mom noticed he wasn't using as much language during that session as he was here at school. She thought we needed the therapist to be right here at school with him helping him use language with other children. Because of that, she arranged lots of meetings with Daniel's early-on coordinator in this building. His mom wanted the coordinator to see how his therapy could happen in the place where Daniel was most communicative. Eventually we had regular visits from the speech therapist.

At one point, the speech therapist wanted us to use an augmented speech board for Daniel. The device was about the size of a cracker box; it had large buttons in rows. Each button had a little space in the front of it where you could insert a picture showing an object like a cracker, juice, the toilet, and so on. We could program each button to say the word or phrase recorded by a familiar voice saying whatever words we wanted Daniel to learn to say. We had words in it like *Daniel*, *juice, more, cracker, my turn, your turn, please, thank you*, and things like that. The idea was that the board was supposed to move with the child around the classroom. If he was standing at the computer and he wanted a turn, he was supposed to push the "my turn" button in the hopes that by hearing the word he would try to repeat it.

"Juice" was a big issue because we always wanted him to get enough juice. We also had to make sure we didn't give too much, because then his glucose level went up. Usually two small cups of juice followed by water was right for Daniel. He had to remember which button to push on the board unless a child nearby would figure out what he needed and say, "Oh, you want this. Push this button. Juice, this one says juice."

We only used that board for about 2 weeks because we noticed Daniel stopped saying the words. He would push the button and look. He wouldn't verbalize the word. We were also concerned that the board became a great toy for the other children. They would push those buttons to get it to work, but we noticed that when this happened, they stopped looking at Daniel. They wanted the board but lost interest in interacting with him. Our goal was to transfer his language progress to the social setting and get him to use words with his peers, but the board wasn't helping. His mom agreed, "That's not working; try something else."

About then we realized we were already using a picture education system with another child who needed help with language in the afternoon class. It was a set of small laminated pictures with a word under each. The pictures attached to a Velcro board, so we could select what we needed quickly. For example, if it were time for Daniel to wash his hands, I could grab the "wash hands" picture, show it to him, and encourage him to say the words. When we used that, Daniel actually did exactly what our goal was: He'd take the picture, say the word, hand it back, and go wash his hands. That worked better for encouraging verbalizing.

Social Strengths

Daniel was quite happy to come to school; he rarely cried, and when he did, he was quickly comforted. He made a lot of friends. Daniel was a very social person, so there were daily social interactions for him. One time the physical therapist brought a special cube chair for Daniel to sit in. We were finding that at group time, when all the children sat on the floor, Daniel was having a difficult time sitting because his torso muscles were weak; he actually fell over. The chair was to help him sit upright. The other children accepted that it was Daniel's special chair. We often saw another child pat the chair and call, "Daniel, come to your chair." They would drag it to him or walk him to the chair. There was all kinds of camaraderie around him. Another little boy, Julian, took to him strongly. Everyday he would announce, "Daniel is my friend." He didn't want to share him with anyone else. Daniel was pleased.

Testing Daniel's blood became routine for everyone in the class. The first few times, we did it as part of a large-group demonstration. After that, we did it more during the choice portion of the day. If we were reading a book with Daniel and a small group of children, we'd say, "It's time to test you, Daniel." He would just put his finger out and life would go on. Sometimes a few children would walk over and stare and want to watch. Then we'd say, "Remember what we are doing? We are testing Daniel's blood. Why are we doing it? To see how much glucose is in there. And whose fingers do we test? Daniel, only Daniel."

I always wonder how children are going to interact with each other. Well, Daniel, who had lots of physical limitations, ended up with a best friend, Julian, who was the most physically active child in class. What connected them was baseball. They both loved sports. I knew Julian watched baseball with his grandfather frequently. One day I mentioned to them both that Daniel went to all his brothers' soccer games, and that became their connection. The first day that connection was evident was when they were playing catch with a soft football in the gym. Daniel always missed the catch, but Julian ran, picked it up, then handed it to him over and over. Daniel and Julian also became really good at the computer, moving the mouse and making things happen on the screen. They would use the computer as a social activity, a time to be buddies.

I think Daniel's big strength was his love for people. In our class he was a member of a small group who had snack together every day. Julian was in that group, too, and those were the children with whom he really connected. When he was deciding which activity to do, he'd find one of his friends and go to them. I have a great picture of Daniel and Julian, all dressed up in the pretend play area. Julian was wearing everything that Daniel had given him to put on, like a vest, a coat, a hat, and gloves.

Daniel also knew which of the children in the class were most receptive to him. If a child he didn't play with very often did something he didn't like, he would push that child away, give a look, and say "no." But if it were one of the kids he was friends with, he'd take it a little bit longer. That was interesting to me because I think he was really learning to read social cues.

Strengthening the Home–School Connection

When Daniel's mom began to leave him with us for the whole morning, we needed consistent daily information that would help monitor Daniel. We had lots of questions such as: If he didn't drink juice at snack time, was that okay? What was his glucose level when he came to school? Should we test him as soon as he got here? How much should we encourage him to eat?

We quickly worked out an effective communication system that we called a daily information sheet. His mom wrote us information on one side, and we recorded for her on the other side. I sent home about a 100 copies with Daniel's mom [see Figure 9.2]. Every day when Daniel arrived, we'd pull the sheet from his backpack and hang it on the refrigerator as a reminder.

We found we were more consistent if we assigned one adult specifically to watch Daniel at mealtime, record what he ate, and be responsible for sending the information sheet home that day. We learned to write down specific foods and amounts; for example, "Daniel ate two saltine crackers and drank two 3-oz.cups of orange juice." Being consistent with that routine was often a challenge, especially when there were new adults in the classroom or special events going on. On Daniel's arrival, along with the information sheet, the glucose kit had to come out of the backpack. It's medical and has needles in it, so we couldn't leave it in his locker down at the children's level. It was put in the same safe

Figure 9.2. Daniel's daily information.

From Home	*From School*
Today's date _____	Today's date _____
Today for breakfast Daniel ate:	Today in school Daniel ate:
_____	_____
_____	_____
_____	_____
_____	_____
_____	_____
_____	_____
_____	
Today Daniel was tested at (time) _____, and his number was _____.	We tested Daniel at (time) _____, and his number was _____.
Today Daniel needs to eat:	This is what he ate and drank today at school:
_____	
_____	_____
_____	_____
_____	_____
_____	_____
_____	_____
	_____
Other advice:	_____
_____	
_____	Other information we want to share with you:
_____	
_____	_____
_____	_____
_____	_____
	_____
I can be reached today at _____	_____
_____,	_____
phone _____ until	_____
_____.	_____
Signed _____	Signed _____

accessible place in the classroom and went home with him every day. That routine became a system that worked very well for us.

Informing Other Parents in the Program

I thought it was important that we give the other parents information about Daniel's special condition, to help them feel comfortable with it. I thought families needed to know so that if their children talked about it, parents could be matter-of-fact with them. I got a pamphlet from the American Diabetes Association, and we sent it home to all our families. I attached a cover letter from me saying essentially, "Here's some information about juvenile diabetes. In case your child talks about this, here's what we're doing. Here are some tips about how you can talk to your child about Daniel." The tips included letting children know that only Daniel's finger would be pricked, no one else's. We also included the words we were using in school to talk about these things. This was the way we educated our families.

I often had parents come in voluntarily to work in the program or to help out on a field trip. In these circumstances, Daniel's tests were seen as very natural. Parents never questioned; they knew about Daniel's testing. Parents reported to me that they heard, "Today Miss Meyers pricked Daniel's finger." They knew what their child had seen, and everyone was fine with that.

Strategies We Used with Daniel

During play time, the children made their own choices about activities, but in Daniel's case we tried to involve him in activities he didn't want to do, because we knew they would help his skill development. We actively invited him to participate in fine-motor activities by saying, "Daniel, come on, it's your turn to string beads" or "It's time to come put your fingers in the modeling dough."

Daniel was the first child I had experience with who had such difficulty walking. I was worried because I didn't want adults to have to carry him all the time. I tried to be aware of how much I was having him move from one place to another. I looked into his daily routine and learned that after dressing and getting ready for school each day, Daniel would walk to the car, ride in a car seat for about 20 minutes, walk about 200 yards up the sloping sidewalk from the parking lot, enter the building, go up five steps and down two hallways before he even got to the classroom. I had to remind myself he had only been walking for about 3 months when he started school. He must have been exhausted by the time he got here.

I considered what I could do to make his journeys less demanding. When we started our morning in the gym, we expected the children to walk up the 10 steps to get to our classroom. I realized that was too much for Daniel. So we started to have his small group take the elevator instead of the stairs. Other days we'd have them use the stairs as a physical activity. When he was tired, he also needed help climbing the steps from the playground. We'd ask a teacher to hold his hand on the stairs.

Our class was used to taking frequent walking field trips to investigate the neighborhood. I had to really think about Daniel and the amount of walking he was able to do. I considered how frequently we could schedule those walking field trips. I also decided to modify the field trip schedule to include only very short distances, such as across the street or to the park nearby. We always had an adult specifically assigned to Daniel who knew he walked slowly and would support him if he needed to stop. Many of the other children were ready to run ahead. But Daniel usually needed to take his time, and he was always the last one to arrive.

Another strategy we used with Daniel was reading books about diabetes to the children. Some of the books were actually for 4- to 8-year-olds, so we eliminated some words and simplified the story, talking about the pictures. They were on the shelf all year. We also had books that featured children with Down syndrome, like *Dustin's Big School Day*.

A strategy we used with all the children was making "All About Me" books. For Daniel, the goal of making his book was to make him feel comfortable with who he was. We took pictures of him in his special chair, drinking juice, playing at the computer, getting his blood tested, and having his hand held while walking up the stairs. As I mentioned before, we also included pictures his mom shared with us about him as a baby with his family.

Another strategy we tried worked better than I anticipated. I brought a child-sized walker into the classroom and encouraged children to practice walking with it. Daniel was the best at it. His mom told us, "Oh, yes, Daniel used to walk with a walker for months." That walker proved to be an important way that Daniel could show his skill. I was able to tell the children, "Daniel had some experience with this. Daniel used one of these before his legs were strong enough to hold him up." That raised Daniel in everyone's eyes.

That spring, Daniel had to make a transition from my classroom to another classroom for our summer program. His new teacher and I met several times during April and early May to discuss Daniel's needs, habits, goals, and procedures. I introduced her to his support team. I introduced

Daniel to the summer teacher, and his mom took him to explore his new classroom. By the time the summer class began, Daniel, his mom, and his new teacher seemed comfortable with the change.

Lessons I Learned

After working with Daniel and his team, I now say to families, "My specialty is not special education; I don't have a special education degree. But here's what I do have, and here's what I'm willing to do for your child." In general, collaborating with support specialists has been wonderful. It's okay that I don't know about some things, because I have someone who can help to find the answers.

On complex and difficult days, it sometimes feels like it would be a lot easier not to have children with special needs in my classroom. Dealing with the special education support people was challenging at times. When I talk with other teachers about it, they say, "Oh, when you get a child who has all those specialists, it is so much work." But, you know, I really mourned having to give Daniel up at the end of the schoolyear. There was a special connection I made with that child, and I wanted to be sure that his next teacher felt the same way. I think it's really hard, because you can't guarantee that. I feel invested in all of my children, but those, like Daniel, who have the specialness about them, they're tougher to let go.

Epilogue

Daniel is now nearly 5 years old and continues in the same school half-days, 4 days a week, with a different teacher. He has made good strides in his ability to communicate, speaking in short but complete sentences. He continues to have regular services from his speech therapists, physical therapist, and occupational therapist. His family has also enrolled Daniel in a PPI class, which he attends most afternoons.

INFORMATION FOR EDUCATORS ABOUT DOWN SYNDROME AND JUVENILE DIABETES

Down Syndrome

Down syndrome (DS) is one of the most common genetic disorders. It occurs in 1 of every 800 to 1,000 births. Most cases are caused by the presence of an extra copy of chromosome 21. Children born with Down syndrome have mild to moderate mental disability. Other common features of DS include poor muscle tone (known as hypotonia, which diminishes with age and early intervention), short stature, a small nose with a flat nasal bridge, small skin folds on the inner corner of the eyes (called epicanthic folds), dry skin, immune-system suppression, developmental delays (e.g., in major motor skills and feeding skills), and speech difficulties. Medical problems associated with Down syndrome are congenital heart defects (40%–60%), gastrointestinal defects; ear, nose, and throat problems; orthopedic problems; and endocrine disorders (e.g., thyroid disease). Some children with DS have vision problems (e.g., congenital cataracts) or hearing loss. With early detection, however, most medical problems are treatable, and most individuals with DS lead healthy, full lives (Kozma, 1986; Spiker & Hopmann, 1997).

Juvenile Diabetes

Juvenile diabetes, also known as type 1 diabetes, is a disease in which the pancreas fails to produce the hormone insulin. The results are life-threateningly high blood-sugar levels. Children with juvenile diabetes must take multiple insulin shots daily for the rest of their lives. The disease is estimated to strike 1 in 500 children across the country. There are an estimated 800,000 people with type 1 diabetes in the United States. When the disease is controlled with diet and treatment, children with the illness can lead as active a life as any other child. Trying to impress children with the seriousness of the disease without worrying them too much is difficult. Keeping blood-sugar levels normal requires balancing food intake with insulin injections. Children with JD must control their intake of sugar but also need constant snacks to keep their blood-sugar level stable. Predicting how the body will react to different stimuli is by no means a perfect science. An illness, physical exercise, a delay in snack time, as well as a host of other variables, can alter blood-sugar levels. A major drawback to injecting insulin is that glucose levels can swing up high right after an injection and down low before the next. Frequent monitoring is critical (Lombardi, 1998).

Advocates for children with the disease report that there appears to be an increase in the number of children with JD, but advances in technology are permitting children to better manage the illness. With the rising number of cases, reports of problems with the way some settings handle diabetic children's needs are also evident. Sometimes students are prevented from going on class trips, participating in sports, or in some cases having a snack or glucose tablets in their classrooms when their blood sugar is low because of policies restricting food to the cafeteria. Some children are refused permission to get water or to go to the lavatory, which is necessary when blood-sugar levels rise (McCarthy, 1999).

The good news is that researchers are working on a vaccine for diabetes, which might someday prevent the disease in newborns, much the same as shots for measles or hepatitis B. They are also working to find the cause or trigger of the disease (McNamara, 2000).

HINTS FOR SUCCESS

The following strategies can help adults working with a child like Daniel successfully include him or her in everyday classroom activities.

1. View children with mental disability or chronic disease as children first and foremost. Focus on their similarities to other children rather than their differences.
2. In presenting tasks, focus on each component of the task clearly, while reducing outside stimuli that may distract the child from learning.
3. Provide a lot of practice using short but frequent sessions to ensure the child is mastering the skills before moving on to more complex skills.
4. Facilitate transfer of learning from school to home. Provide meaningful information about the child's progress in the early childhood program to the child and family.
5. Recognize children with mental disabilities for their own accomplishments rather than comparing them to peers without disabilities.
6. Employ cooperative learning strategies wherever possible to promote effective learning. Establish peer buddies or cross-age tutoring.
7. For children with juvenile diabetes, monitor the child's behavior before meals or snacks. Make sure food is served on schedule. Keep a source of sugar readily available.
8. Use the Internet to help you keep up to date on the facts about Down syndrome and juvenile diabetes. Contact professional organizations related to each condition for further information.

QUESTIONS FOR DISCUSSION

1. In what was the home visit strategy valuable for this teacher? What information did she learn?
2. Compare Daniel's experience with juvenile diabetes to that of someone you know who has a similar condition. How is it the same; how is it different?

3. If you were the parent of another child in this teacher's class, what are some of the questions you would have for the teacher regarding Daniel?
4. What resources did this teacher use that proved successful with Daniel?

RESOURCES FOR EDUCATORS AND PARENTS

Organizations

American Diabetes Association
National Service Center
1660 Duke Street
Alexandria, VA 22314
Phone: (800) 232-3472, (703) 549-1500
Website: hhttp://www.diabetes.org (retrieved 5/18/01)

Juvenile Diabetes Foundation International
432 Park Avenue South
New York, NY 10016
Phone: (800) 533-2873, (212) 889-7575
Website: http://www.jdf.org (retrieved 5/18/01)

March of Dimes Birth Defects Foundation
1275 Mamaroneck Avenue
White Plains, NY 10605
Phone: (888) 663-4637
Website: http://www.modimes.org

National Diabetes Information Clearinghouse
One Information Way
Bethesda, MD 20892
Phone: (301) 654-3327
Website: http://www.niddk.nih.gov/health/diabetes/ndic.htm
(retrieved 5/18/01)

National Down Syndrome Congress
700 Peachtree-Dunwoody Road NE
Building 5, Suite 100
Atlanta, GA 30328–1662
Phone: (800) 232-6372
Website: http://www.ndsccenter.org

National Down Syndrome Society
666 Broadway

New York, NY 10012
Phone: (800) 221-4602
Website: http://www.ndss.org

National Institute of Child Health and Human Development
PO Box 3006
Rockville, MD 20847
Phone: (800) 370-2943
Website: http://www.nichd.nih.gov

Books and Articles for Adults

Anderson, W., Chitwood, S., & Hayden, D. (1997). *Negotiating the special education maze: A guide for parents and teachers.* Bethesda, MD: Woodbine House.
Betschart, J. (1999). *Diabetes care for babies, toddlers, and preschoolers: A reassuring guide for parents.* Minneapolis, MN: Chronimed.
Bruni, M. (1998). *Fine motor skills in children with Down syndrome: A guide for parents and professionals.* Bethesda, MD: Woodbine House.
Johnson, R. W., IV, & Johnson, C. (1994). *Managing your child's diabetes.* New York: Master Media.
Loring, G. (1999). *Parenting a diabetic child.* Los Angeles: Lowell House.
   [*A practical guide for parents that gives a spirit of hope.*]
National Institute of Child Health and Human Development. (1995). *Facts about Down syndrome.* Rockville, MD: Author.
   [*Explains the important provisions of the Individuals with Disabilities Education Act (IDEA) in easy-to-understand language.*] Available Online:
   www.nichd.nih.gov/publications/pubs/downsyndrome.
Siminerio, L. (2000). *American Diabetes Association guide to raising a child with diabetes.* Alexandria, VA: American Diabetes Association.
Trainer, M. (1991). *Differences in common: Straight talk on mental retardation, Down syndrome, and life.* Rockville, MD: Woodbine House.
   [*A collection of essays for parents to help them understand the triumphs and challenges of raising a child with a disability.*]
Winders, P. C. (1998). *Gross motor skills in children with down syndrome: A guide for parents and professionals.* Bethesda, MD.: Woodbine House.
   [*A guide for parents and professionals to support children in the gross-motor area, to challenge basic gross motor skills, and to give confidence.*]

Books and Magazines for Children

Betschart, J. (1995). *A magic ride in foozbah-land: An inside look at diabetes.* Minneapolis, MN: Chronimed.
   [*Uses rhymes to teach children ages 3 to 7 causes of diabetes and why they need shots. Audiocassette also available.*]

Carter, A. R. (1997). *Big brother Dustin*. Morton Grove, IL: A. Whitman & Co.
[*A child with Down Syndrome learns to deal with a new baby in his household.*]
Carter, A. R. (1999). *Dustin's big school day*. Morton Grove, IL: A. Whitman & Co.
[*A second-grader with Down syndrome anticipates the arrival of two special guests at school.*]
Gosselin, K. (1998). *Rufus comes home*. Valley Park, MO: JayJo Books.
[*Children aged 3 to 10 will enjoy this tale of a child with diabetes who has a stuffed bear with the same disease.*]
Pirner, C. W. (1991). *Even little kids get diabetes*. Morton Grove, IL: A. Whitman & Co.
[*This book helps children aged 2 to 6 deal with the psychological effects of diabetes.*]

Countdown for Kids: The magazine for kids with diabetes. Published by the Juvenile Diabetes Foundation.

REFERENCES

Kozma, C. (1986) Medical concerns and treatments. In K. Stray-Gundersen (Ed.), *Babies with Down syndrome: A new parents guide*. Kensington, MD: Woodbine House.
Lombardi, K. S. (1998, May 17). Keeping life in balance despite diabetes. *New York Times*, p. 14.
McCarthy, P. (1999, October 10). Dealing with diabetes in school. New York, NY: *New York Times*, p. 14.
McNamara, D. (2000). Overcoming juvenile diabetes with a little planning and high-tech tools. *FDA Consumer*, 34(4), 28–31.
Spiker, D., & Hopmann, M. R. (1997). The effectiveness of early intervention for children with Down syndrome. In M. J. Guralnick (Ed.), *The effectiveness of early intervention* (pp. 271–305). Baltimore: Brookes.

CHAPTER 10

Katherine Mary
The Once-Upon-a-Time Girl

Katherine Mary: Tell me that story, Mama. Tell me the choosing story! Tell me about, "Once upon a time."

Mama: Once upon a time there was a little girl named Katherine Mary. She had a father, a mother, and a grandmother. Her mother was very ill, and her grandmother died. And her father couldn't live at home anymore. So people came and took Katherine Mary to another place to live for a little while.

She went to live in this big building. It had a crib in the middle of a great big room, and at night that is where she slept. During the daytime she walked around and talked to grown-ups whenever she had a chance.

Not far away lived a man and a woman who wanted a child to love. They were looking for a child who needed a mother and father. Some arrangements were made, and Mama and Daddy went to visit this little girl. She had on a red coat and a bonnet, and she loved to talk. They took her out to lunch. I don't think Katherine Mary had ever been out to lunch before. They bought her french fries and a burger. I don't think she had ever eaten french fries before either. She spilled them all over the floor and tossed them across the room. She ate a few, and she ate part of the hamburger. She jabbered most of the time, and her new mother and father couldn't quite understand her. But they thought she was wonderful, and they wanted to choose her to be their own little girl. They took her back to the big place where she was staying and asked the people there if Katherine Mary could come to their house to live. Well, a week later they said "yes." So the mother and father went and picked up Katherine Mary and brought her home. She had on a bright chartreuse-colored dress and a pair of brown shoes.

She came in the house, and she sucked her thumb and looked around. She was pretty scared. The first thing she said was, "Are you going to take me back?" Her new mother said, "No. You're our little girl now. We'll never take you back. I'm your mother now, and this is your daddy now, and you're here to stay with us."

Katherine Mary asks for this story often, even now, 28 years after it happened. What follows is the true story of that little girl's early childhood years as told by her mother and her sister.

Looking at pictures in a family photo album, Katherine Mary's mother points to a black-and-white photo of a smiling preschooler sitting on an older woman's lap outdoors. Even though it is a still photograph, you can see the energy in the child. She is looking away from the camera with her arms and legs in motion. It's not hard to imagine that as soon as the picture was taken, she was off her grandmother's lap and on the move.

HER MOTHER TELLS KATHERINE MARY'S STORY

Here is Katherine Mary a few weeks after we got her. Her hair was honey blonde with some brown in it. It was very heavy hair, whereas mine is very fine. She has greenish-blue eyes. People in our family have mostly brown eyes, but my dad has greenish-blue eyes, which she found very satisfying. She liked it that her eyes were the same color as her grandpa's even though she knew she was adopted.

As you can see, Katherine Mary was constantly active. Her body motions were not really controlled. If you held her closely in your lap, you could anticipate getting some bruises because her elbows moved, her arms moved, her head moved, and she would clutch at you with her hands. She wanted to be held, but she could not control her body very well. Even in her sleep, she was moving and flapping the whole time. She talked in her sleep, too. She just kept going 24 hours a day.

Katherine Mary was almost 4 when we adopted her. She was presented to us as a normally developing 4-year-old with a lazy eye. That's why she was wearing glasses. We were allowed to meet her once before we adopted her. We took her out to lunch. She did not know how to eat with silverware. So we assisted her and did some partial feeding. Her behavior was extreme (throwing food, mushing it with her hands), but we thought that was just because she was in a strange situation and we were new adults she had never met before.

On her health appraisal form, there was a question mark in the column headed "mental health." I thought at the time that she was just too young for this to have been assessed. The physical health sections were marked "normal." I found out much later that there was a lot of medical history that was not included in that paperwork. If it had been there, even the most uninformed adult would have figured that something was seriously wrong with this youngster.

First Days

A week after our lunch, we picked her up and were surprised to find that Katherine Mary had been kept in a jail cell with a crib in it and nothing else. It was a completely austere environment. We were told that the county had set this up as a temporary facility due to overcrowding. They didn't have anywhere else to put her.

She was quite delighted to leave. She didn't want to stay. She was not attached to anybody there; as far as I could tell, she had no relationship with any of her caregivers at the time we picked her up. She ran straight for the car.

When we brought her home, Katherine Mary didn't have any clothes and I didn't know what size she was. We took her to Dillard's Department Store, which was one of the nice department stores in town. It's a funny story, but I went in with Katherine Mary to try to get her to try on some things to figure out sizes. She got away from me two or three times, and in the 45 minutes we were there she knocked over four mannequins.

She emptied out shelf upon shelf of stuff. Every time I turned my back, she would scoop, scoop, and then run all over. My husband and I had to keep chasing her. We gave up trying to buy. We got underwear and some socks and did some estimates on the other things. It took three clerks and two parents to get enough so that this child would have something to wear the next day because she literally had only what she stood up in. It was funny and horrifying at the same time. Incidents like that were fairly typical in her early childhood period, and we gradually learned how to help her behave better in public. But there's no forgetting that first time!

It was obvious that Katherine Mary had not been to a store before. She lacked experience in other areas, too. Her language was very limited. She did not pronounce words clearly, and her vocabulary was minimal. Another thing we had to do right away was teach her how to eat and teach her about foods. She did not know how to eat with a spoon or a fork. She recognized mashed potatoes and eggs. I don't think she recognized any other vegetables or meats. Everything appeared to be new to her.

As soon as we could, we took Katherine Mary to our family doctor. The doctor said she had many signs of malnutrition. There were cracks in her mouth and at the corner of her eyes. Her hair was broken off in places. She had scabby sores on her body and scars that looked like burns. Her clothing had covered these, and we hadn't seen them until her first bath. She had vision problems, too, and is actually legally blind in one eye. Katherine Mary also wet the bed every night (that lasted until she was 6 or 7).

We discovered that unless you touched Katherine Mary, she didn't seem to recognize that a direction applied to her. As a result, she did not comply with requests like, "Come to the bathtub." I mean, ordinary routine events all required physical intervention and support from her dad and me.

Katherine Mary was so very active. At the same time, her motor skills were very poor. She didn't run very well, and she was truly clumsy.

It was heartbreaking to deal with all of this and exhausting to keep up with her. It did not take long for us to realize that there was a lot going on with this child and that we couldn't address everything on our own.

Early Interventions

Within a week of having her at home, we began getting help with Katherine Mary. We went to the pediatrician and an eye specialist. We took her to the intermediate school district to be assessed for special education services. She qualified for the special education pre-primary program but could not begin going there until the fall, which was several months away.

We did all kinds of things to enhance Katherine Mary's motor skills. We went swimming as a family at the YMCA. She took individual lessons, too. We had her do some simple gymnastics, just to get her using her body in fun situations. We went ice-skating. We did both individualized activities plus things in groups. Even though she behaved oddly in the group, she liked being with the other kids. Eventually she acquired enough skill that her coordination improved a little and so did her balance.

We also sought psychological support for her. We hired a social worker who did play therapy with her until she was 10 years old. Unfortunately, Katherine Mary was like a black hole emotionally. She just couldn't get enough attention, and it wasn't possible to give her enough love. Regardless of how many people gave her attention and love, there wasn't enough for her to feel satisfied or filled up.

More than one psychologist observed that Katherine Mary had little understanding of cause and effect and that she was not developing a conscience. Thus she had little understanding of right and wrong and few behavior controls of her own.

In time, we had her cognitive functioning assessed. We discovered she had an IQ between 77 and 80, depending on when she took the test. (She was tested more than once.) This was just a little above the score that signifies mental retardation.

Support from Family and Friends

I must say we had great support from my parents in terms of both moral support and financial needs. Katherine Mary had so many medical expenses, plus her child-care arrangements, therapy, tutoring, and recreational activities. Her glasses alone were a terrific expense. I bought frames by the dozen because she broke them so often. My parents helped a lot with those costs.

Katherine Mary drove my parents to distraction. She was not obedient, and she was not polite. Yet they included her in everything. She was treated as part of the family. Because my parents could not run after her and be right there every minute, they could not handle her physically. I mean, they were older and just couldn't deal with that, but they were very loving and supportive of her when we visited or when they came here.

My friends often gave me the support I needed to continue to parent. Most important, they treated Katherine Mary respectfully. I mean they treated her like a person, not a problem or an object. They treated her like a human being who had feelings. They didn't stereotype her, which I think had a humanizing effect on her and on me.

We had one particular family friend, Elizabeth, who ate dinner with us every Monday night. We had been doing this for years, and it continued after Katherine Mary became part of our lives. Elizabeth was a single woman who had no children. When she came over, she gave Katherine Mary her undivided attention. She would be so accepting of Katherine Mary, so supportive of her. Katherine Mary could be very demanding, and Elizabeth took all that in stride. We colored Easter eggs, we made pictures, we played games—all the things families do with their kids—and Elizabeth was part of that, too. She never criticized. Though I must admit one time when Katherine Mary was particularly difficult, after we finally got her to bed, Elizabeth said to me, "I always wanted to be married and have kids, but I think there could be some things harder than being single." That's the only thing that even came close to a criticism, but I haven't forgotten it. Katherine Mary had been particularly obnoxious on that occasion and exhausting—very exhausting. But I think she enriched Elizabeth's life and gave her new insights and things to think about. In turn, Katherine Mary really doted on her.

Katherine Mary was able to attend the Sunday School at our church. I know it was really hard for people to handle her there, and I'm pretty sure the Sunday School teachers planned who was going to take Katherine Mary and how they were going to cope with her. They never kicked her out. We really felt supported there.

In the 10 years that Katherine Mary lived at home, I had 2 weekends off. A person with a special education background from our church offered to take her for those weekends to give us a break at home. That was a marvelous gift of time. It gave us a chance to catch our breath.

Katherine Mary in Child Care

During her first year with us, Katherine Mary went to a child-care center because my husband and I both worked. This was a highly supportive setting. The staff was tremendously helpful. They were consistent in their expectations and very patient with her. It must have been difficult for them because she was not at all compliant. She would take things away from the other children, and she would hide things in the room. She disrupted group time and had frequent temper tantrums. One day she soiled herself at naptime and wiped the feces all over herself, the cot, and the floor. Through all of this the staff was accepting of her as a person but firm in terms of setting boundaries. I felt comfortable with that and relieved that she had good care away from home.

Things came up that first year that took all of us by surprise. The most vivid incident involved a time when the center invited a police officer to talk with the children. As part of the visit, the officer invited the children to climb into the backseat of his squad car. Katherine Mary became totally distraught. She kept saying that if you got into the car, "You will never see your mother again." She was convinced that any child who got into that car would be taken away forever. This was very real to her. She carried on with such force that she managed to keep the children away from the vehicle. The whole class fell apart. Kids were crying, and Katherine Mary was hysterical. She didn't want the police officer touching anyone, including the teachers. She was screaming and pushing to keep them all away. The director called me immediately, and I left what I was doing and went right over there. The staff explained everything to me. I sat down with Katherine Mary and reassured her that the police officer would not carry her away. The police officer was not going to take her or anybody else. She wasn't so sure, so I said, "Daddy and I can stop this from happening. This will not happen to you. You are our little girl, and no one can take you away."

That theme persisted for many years. Almost every morning Katherine Mary would ask, "Are you going to be here when I get back? Am I staying here?" I reassured her and made up the "choosing story" to get the message across at times when she wasn't upset. I told that story many times to reassure her and help her feel like she was a specially chosen child whom we loved.

I think the staff handled the police-officer situation with amazing poise. They were extremely patient and also very skilled. They had a strong commitment to helping her and supporting us as parents.

The center was a lifeline for our family—a respite for a few hours each day. It was so hard keeping up with Katherine Mary. I couldn't have done it 24 hours a day every day.

When Katherine Mary became too old to go to the center anymore, we hired someone to stay with her after school. We could not leave her unsupervised ever—her behavior was extreme. This was true as long as she was living at home. We had a lot of turnover in this regard. People had a hard time coping with all her various challenges.

Formal Schooling

Formal schooling for Katherine Mary began with her enrollment in a pre-primary special education program in the fall. She still went to the day-care center in the morning, and then we transported her to the special education setting in the afternoon. There was no bus service, so I left work each day to get her over there. Then either my husband or I picked her up at the end of the 2-hour session and transported her back to the center until one of us got out of work at 5:00.

This program was entirely different from the one at the center. We had really divergent ideas about what she should be working on. They wanted her to write her name; I wanted her to learn to eat with a spoon. She could hardly run, and they began working on things like hopping and tumbling. She couldn't tear paper, and they wanted her to use the scissors. She did work with an occupational therapist on some eye–hand coordination, and that was good.

She went to kindergarten the next year, but within 2 weeks she was back in the pre-primary program. The kindergarten teacher just had no way of handling her acting-out behavior. In kindergarten, she didn't comply, she didn't sit in her seat, and she didn't stand in line. There was no aide. They had no resource room. The school decided she would be better off back in special education. They called me on the telephone. They didn't even have the courtesy to speak to me in person and tell me their decision. They didn't ask; they just said, "This is how it's going to be."

She went straight from the pre-primary special education program to first grade and then to second grade in our local public school. In first grade, she was off in a corner, separated from the rest of the group. They said it was so she could concentrate better and maybe that's true, but I think it was also easier for them to ignore her and keep her from disrupting things.

Her second-grade teacher was very good. She treated Katherine Mary as if she had potential. She had clear expectations and knew how to break tasks into smaller components to make it easier for her to learn. The school also provided Katherine Mary with 15 minutes of individualized physical education each day. She and the physical education teacher worked on her fundamental motor skills, and she did make progress. She became more efficient in things like walking and running and what you might call daily use of the body.

Third grade was a nightmare. The children bullied Katherine Mary, especially on the playground. She became a class scapegoat. She came home with torn clothes and bruises. The children threw her boots in the garbage, they cut her hair. No adult intervened. Of course, she carried on a lot and egged the bullies on, but no teacher came to her rescue, not once that whole year. I went to the school several times to talk about it, but the problems continued. That same year, I actually hired a retired teacher to come to her school to tutor her in reading during the schoolday. Her classroom teacher did not provide the necessary individualized instruction. He told us he didn't know what to do with Katherine Mary—he had no idea how to reach her. He focused on keeping her contained.

We sent her to a different school for fourth and fifth grades. We needed to at least know she was safe. Her fourth-grade teacher deserves particular mention. She was superb. She took her profession seriously and was determined that Katherine Mary would learn to read, which she did. Having this child in her class was difficult, but she made a great effort. She even sent home a "glad note" saying that Katherine Mary had done something correctly. That was such a big deal to all of us. We had never received one of those before. I observed Katherine Mary in that classroom. She was sitting under her desk, but she was not making noise and she even answered a question. We decided with the teacher that it really didn't matter if she was sitting under a desk as long as she worked. It took a skilled and empathic professional to handle a child under a desk, but that year Katherine Mary made great progress. I will always be grateful for that teacher's attitude and her skills.

This papier-mâché sculpture is so typical of her at that time (fourth grade). It is a self-portrait of Katherine Mary in action with arms and legs askew [see Figure 10.1].

Katherine Mary was on Ritalin from first grade through the time she left the local public schools (at the end of fifth grade). The doctor prescribed a dosage that just cooled her off a bit. I didn't want her to have so much that she became a zombie. We gave her just enough to move her down from an impossibly active child to a highly active one.

School Conferences

Going to school conferences was an ordeal. It was so upsetting that I would not go home for dinner beforehand; my stomach was churning too much. Afterwards I would drive around and try to pull myself together before heading home. Mostly I'd go in and listen for 30 minutes about all the terrible things my child had done. Many teachers seemed to blame me for her behavior and wanted to know what I was going to do to get her to listen better in the classroom.

The poorer teachers just wanted to get rid of her. I mean, their ultimate goal was to get her out of their hair. The better teachers felt guilty that they didn't know how to handle things more effectively. I found myself comforting them and trying to offer emotional support because I knew how difficult it all was. In the end I gave the same message to each teacher along the way. I'd say, "You don't have to like her, but you do have to teach her. We don't have anyplace else to go."

Figure 10.1. Katherine Mary's sculpture of herself with legs askew.

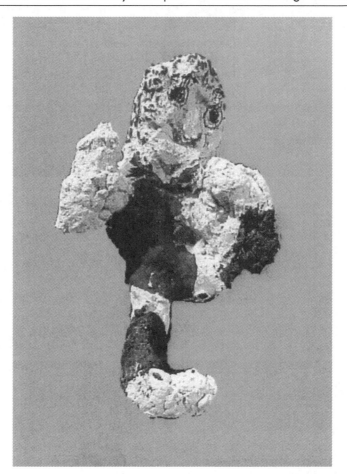

I pushed the system relentlessly. I know I gave them a hard time because I thought of her as a person, not a case. She was a person who could read if somebody would teach her to read. She was a person who could do mathematics if they'd teach her to add and subtract. She was a person who could know things, feel things, and do things. I got angry with them. Perhaps it was sheer stubbornness, but she was a living being, and I thought she deserved some dignity in life, no matter how tough it was on anyone else.

I don't think anybody was mean-hearted. They were exasperated, they were exhausted, they were frustrated, and they didn't know what to do. Many of them also didn't take the time to find out what to do. Mostly they complained. In the meantime, I was scrambling to learn things myself. All those years I was going to the library, calling professional organizations, searching for literature that might help. I kept passing along what I learned to her teachers, but they seldom passed anything on to me. I know they were having a bad time. But it was miserable being treated as though it was my fault or as though I was a bad parent. Some treated me like I was fool or just plain incompetent. If they were having such a hard time, couldn't they surmise we were having an equally hard time raising this child?

HER SISTER TALKS ABOUT GROWING UP WITH KATHERINE MARY

Katherine Mary has always been my sister (she was 5 when I was born). I don't know any other way of life. It's not strange or unusual; it's just how it is.

I think the good times are harder to remember than the bad times because the good times are not big events. Bad times were events with Katherine Mary (like when she got beat up, or when she hurt my mom or me, or when she got lost in the neighborhood). Good times were when she was happy or content. That didn't happen often. Good times were when my mom didn't have to run after her; my dad wasn't worrying about her; she was having fun or someone liked her. It might be as simple as getting through a whole meal without a tantrum or playing for 10 minutes in a row.

People's Reactions to Katherine Mary

Katherine Mary had one friend in the neighborhood. Rosalie also had a disability. It was a good time when they played together. It was great that someone her own age was nice to her. No other child who was nice to her wasn't my friend already. That friendship lasted until Rosalie moved away when Katherine Mary was 10.

Katherine Mary is loud and disruptive, so people are often looking at her. She will yell, scream, and throw tantrums; that is embarrassing sometimes. But Katherine Mary's slowness and her inability to learn have never embarrassed me. That's just part of who she is.

People say things that can really hurt. I've heard people say loud enough for us to hear that they would never let their child act like that. They have no clue as to how things are. When I was in elementary school, some of the adults said things to me like, "If your mother stayed home, Katherine Mary wouldn't act that way" or "She needs a good spanking." Believe me, just spanking Katherine Mary or having my mom spend every day at home with her would not have changed things. It's interesting that adults would say those kinds of things to a young child, though.

People aren't tolerant of certain disabilities. Maybe if she had been in a wheelchair, used a cane, or had a hearing aid, people would have been more understanding. But I think kids like Katherine Mary who are slow to learn, hyperactive, and not very cute get a lot of resentment and anger heaped on them.

Going to School in Katherine Mary's Footsteps

Since Katherine Mary went to school ahead of me, everyone knew me as her sibling. We had many of the same teachers in school. They had very negative memories of dealing with her. From the school principal to the janitor, everyone thought of Katherine Mary as a terror. And she was, no doubt about it. I knew this and was very careful and sensitive to what people thought about me. I tried to make them happy.

At first, I could tell that the teachers walked on eggshells around me. But once they got to know me, it was fine.

Other children on the playground or other children I wasn't friends with would say mean things to me about Katherine Mary. Those remarks always upset me. When I think about Katherine Mary at school, I think about how mean kids were and about the teachers who never said or did anything to stop it. I think they figured Katherine Mary got what she deserved.

I didn't realize how important it was for me to be thought about in my own right until something happened in the fourth grade. All my teachers until then had had Katherine Mary in their classrooms. Mrs. Tea was new to the school, and she was my teacher. I felt like I was starting with a clean slate. One day Mrs. Tea asked me to stay for a few minutes after school. She sat me down in a little chair and said, "I hear your sister is going to a residential school. That will be good thing for you." I was so surprised! I assumed Mrs. Tea didn't know anything about Katherine Mary. Of course, now I realize the other teachers must have warned her about us, but in my head I was unaware that this teacher knew anything about her. I was so mad. I was mad that she knew. I wanted this to be a teacher who saw me for myself with no shadow, no preconceived ideas about my family or me. Now it was spoiled.

Friends

Certainly for my friends, having someone with a handicap in their lives has made them more understanding of people who have disabilities.

I went to the same school from kindergarten through high school. The friends I had in kindergarten were many of the same friends I had at graduation. They would come to our house, and I would tell them about Katherine Mary ahead of time. I would say, "Don't be afraid. Don't laugh." I tried to prepare them for her. They were kind for the most part; they accommodated to her abilities. They were my friends, and they treated her nicely because she was my sister. Children her own age were so cruel to her, and the teachers were mean to her, too.

At my graduation, my friends that were true to me went up to her and said, "Nice to see you." "Glad you could make it." It's a pleasure to have you here." Five sentences could make her day. They did that for me, and I know that. They have always been that way.

Impact on Career

I have chosen health care as a career. I work with children with disabilities in a pediatric setting. I think I have more empathy and more concern for that population as a result of living with Katherine Mary.

KATHERINE MARY'S MOTHER CONTINUES THE STORY

As Katherine Mary's developmental problems became more apparent, we tried to get information from the county and the state to get a clearer picture of her background. We kept running into roadblocks, and no one would tell us anything. After several years and many tries, we finally got a court order to get her early health records. Those records showed a pattern of starvation and then hospitalizations to build her back up.

We found out later that she was removed from her family for cause; the problem was abuse and neglect. Apparently she also witnessed a murder, which resulted in her being carried off by the police. Clearly she had been raised in a very violent environment.

I have an abiding anger at the system that (1) lied to us about her background and (2) covered up things that would have helped us to parent Katherine Mary more effectively all those years. I think they were afraid we'd give her back to the state. They didn't know us. We're too stubborn for that. A child isn't a pet from the Humane Society that you pick out and then give back if the going gets rough. I didn't see her as hopeless.

Epilogue

When it came time for Katherine Mary to leave the elementary program and go to middle school, we moved her to a mental health residential treatment center. The state paid for some of her tuition, and we paid the rest. There was no way she could have been successful in school moving from one classroom to another throughout the day. Also, by that time she had begun hurting herself (sometimes scratching herself with a needle or a nail). She was also threatening her younger sister with bodily harm. It was frightening. We realized we needed help beyond what was in place at that point. The residential program was very structured and used many behavior-modification strategies. Children set academic as well as life-skill goals and worked on achieving them, earning various privileges along the way. The ultimate aim was for them to become capable of living in the community independently.

Ultimately, Katherine Mary learned language well. She speaks clearly and has a pretty broad vocabulary. She also learned how to behave with support in a variety of social settings. She can go to church, to the movies, or to the store and behave reasonably well. She can use the telephone, ride a bus, and go out to lunch in a restaurant with me. Katherine Mary can read and do simple math, like adding up the items on a grocery bill. She likes to make things—hooked rugs and afghans. She likes to knit and does that fairly well. She is very good at making models (like planes or plastic ships).

Katherine Mary never developed a notion of cause and effect. She doesn't understand how one event relates to another. So she doesn't understand that if you yell at your boss or if you get nasty with customers or colleagues, you will be fired. She still doesn't know how to get along with other people. As a result, she has been unable to hold a job.

She is living in the community. Her life is marginal, but she has never been in jail and she is not institutionalized. Her income comes from Social Security, and I supplement it as best I can. I still deal with many crises. Yet Katherine Mary is proud that she is living on her own. We have lunch every Saturday and spend holiday time together.

Katherine Mary is invariably cheerful in spite of some pretty tough circumstances. It has been hard for her. She is persistent. She tries and tries in spite of an enormous amount of failure. I think she deserves credit for that.

INFORMATION FOR EDUCATORS ABOUT DISABILITY-RIGHTS LAWS

Katherine Mary began her formal schooling in 1971, 4 years before passage of Public Law 94-142, the Education of the Handicapped Act (EHA). This federal law requires states to provide "a free and appropriate public education" to all school-age children with disabilities. Additionally, it requires every child with a disability to be educated in the least restrictive environment. This means that to the fullest extent possible, the program environment for children with disabilities must be the same as, or similar to, the environment provided for typically developing children. Before that law was passed, schools were not obligated to provide education services to meet the unique needs of children with handicapping conditions in regular classroom environments. Since then, the law has been amended several times.

In 1986, the EHA was amended through Public Law 99-457 to, among other things, lower the age at which children can receive special services to 3 years old. It also established the Handicapped Infants and Toddlers Program (Part H), which is for children who need help from birth to 3 years of age. The amendments of 1990 and 1991 brought about a name change—EHA is now called IDEA, the Individuals with Disabilities Education Act. IDEA requires that all states provide public school education to children with disabilities, no matter how severe their disabilities are, from ages 3 to 21.

Another law, the Rehabilitation Act of 1973 (P.L. 93-112), which was amended in 1992 by P.L. 102-569, also has significance for the rights of children with disabilities. This law prohibits discrimination against persons with disabilities. Furthermore, Section 504 of the act prohibits the exclusion of children with disabilities from programs receiving federal funding simply because they have a disability. Section 504 defines a person with a disability as "any person who (i) has a physical or mental impairment which substantially limits one or more of that person's major life activities, (ii) has a record of such an impairment, or (iii) is regarded as having such an impairment." As a recipient of federal funds, public schools, Head Start programs, and many child-care centers are prohibited from discriminating against children who meet this definition. Such programs must create accommodations to assist children in participating in the daily activities of the program.

The general definition of *disability* has been more specifically described, and children evaluated as having any of the following impairments are defined as needing special education and related services (U.S. Office of Special Education and Rehabilitative Services, 1999):

Deaf
Having a hearing impairment which is so severe that the student is impaired in processing linguistic information through hearing (with or without amplification) and which adversely affects educational performance.

Deaf-blind
Having concomitant hearing and visual impairments which cause such severe communication and other developmental and educational problems that the student cannot be accommodated in special education programs solely for deaf or blind students.

Hard of hearing
Having a hearing impairment, whether permanent or fluctuating, which adversely affects the student's educational performance, but which is not included under the definition of "deaf" in this section.

Mentally retarded
Having significantly subaverage general intellectual functioning, existing concurrently with defects in adaptive behavior and manifested during the developmental period, which adversely affects the child's educational performance.

Multihandicapped
Having concomitant impairments (such as mentally retarded-blind, mentally retarded-orthopedically impaired, etc.), the combination of which causes such severe educational problems that the student cannot be accommodated in special education programs solely for one of the impairments. Term does not include deaf-blind students but does include those students who are severely or profoundly mentally retarded.

Orthopedically impaired
Having a severe orthopedic impairment which adversely affects a student's educational performance. The term includes impairment resulting from congenital anomaly, disease, or other causes.

Other health impaired
Having limited strength, vitality, or alertness due to chronic or acute health problems such as a heart condition, tuberculosis, rheumatic fever, nephritis, asthma, sickle cell anemia, hemophilia, epilepsy, lead poisoning, leukemia, or diabetes which adversely affects the student's educational performance.

Seriously emotionally disturbed
Exhibiting one or more of the following characteristics over a long period of time, to a marked degree, and adversely affecting educational performance: an inability to learn which cannot be explained by intellectual, sensory, or health factors; an inability to build or maintain satisfactory interpersonal relationships with peers and teachers; inappropriate types of behavior or feelings under normal circumstances; a general pervasive mood of unhappiness or depression; or a tendency to develop physical symptoms or fears associated with personal or school problems. This term does not include children who are socially maladjusted, unless they also display one or more of the listed characteristics.

Specific learning disabled
Having a disorder in one or more of the basic psychological processes involved in understanding or in using spoken or written language, which may manifest itself in an imperfect ability to listen, think, speak, read, write, spell, or do mathematical calculations. The term includes such conditions as perceptual handicaps, brain injury, minimal brain dysfunction, dyslexia, and developmental aphasia. The term does not include children who have learning problems which are primarily the result of visual, hearing, or environmental, cultural, or economic disadvantage.

Speech impaired
Having a communication disorder, such as stuttering, impaired articulation, language impairment, or voice impairment, which adversely affects the student's educational performance.

Visually handicapped
Having a visual impairment which, even with correction, adversely affects the student's educational performance. The term includes partially seeing and blind children.

HINTS FOR SUCCESS

With all these laws in place, children with disabilities currently have the right to participate fully in early childhood programs from preschool through the elementary grades; the challenge lies in the execution of the intent of the law in our local communities. Here are some suggestions for how to make a positive translation of the law in your program.

1. Keep informed about organizations and community groups that provide support to children with special needs, their families, and the professionals who work with them.

2. Work closely with parents and other family members to ensure that communication between home and school is open and that strategies are consistent across both environments.
3. Focus on the capabilities of each child as well as the impairments he or she may manifest.
4. Apply strategies you have learned that represent developmentally appropriate practices in early childhood education with all the children in your program.
5. Seek assistance from specialists to create effective strategies for dealing with children's classroom behavior.
6. Take responsibility for the child's functioning in the classroom while the child is there rather than blaming the parents or ignoring the child.
7. Consider children within the context of their family and community as well as in terms of the early childhood environment.
8. Recognize that families need your support as much as their children do.
9. Communicate with the many different professionals who may be involved in meeting a child's educational needs.
10. Join advocacy and support groups that provide information and assistance related to children with special needs.

QUESTIONS FOR DISCUSSION

1. Go back through the narrative in this chapter and find examples of things that are not in keeping with IDEA. What does this tell you about IDEA and the progress we have made regarding children with special needs over the past 20 to 30 years?
2. Read through the definitions of impairments described in this chapter. Review the narrative and identify elements of Katherine Mary's behavior that might be covered by any of the definitions provided.
3. What impact did having a child with special needs seem to have on Katherine Mary's family?
4. Stories that begin with "Once upon a time..." often end with, "and they all lived happily ever after." How well does that ending fit this story?
5. What ethical dilemmas do you think Katherine Mary's teachers encountered?

RESOURCES FOR EDUCATORS AND PARENTS

Books

Allen, K. E., & Schwartz, I. S. (2001). *The exceptional child: Inclusion in early childhood education* (4th ed.). Albany, NY: Delmar.

Chandler, P. A. (1994). *A place for me*. Washington, DC: National Association for the Education of Young Children.

Deiner, P. L. (1993). *Resources for teaching children with diverse abilities: Birth through age eight*. New York: Harcourt Brace Jovanovich.

Organization

National Information Center for Children and Youth (NICHCY)
PO Box 1492
Washington, DC 20013
Phone: (800) 695–0285, (202) 884–8200
Website: www.nichcy.org

REFERENCE

U.S. Office of Special Education and Rehabilitative Services. (1999). *Definitions of impairments addressed by IDEA*. Washingtion, DC: Author, pp. 1–10.

C H A P T E R   1 1

Concluding Our Conversation

Reflections

As we come to the closing of our conversation, it is noteworthy that no two children described in the previous chapters were alike and no single method or approach was best suited for all of them. Each child's story demonstrates a complexity that compels all practitioners to strive to learn about the whole child. Labels by themselves did not reveal clear strategies about how to support the child. Other information and resources were also needed to serve the children effectively.

YOUR ROLES IN SERVING CHILDREN WITH SPECIAL NEEDS

Now that you have read about nine children with special needs who entered early childhood education settings, we would like you to reflect on what you have learned from these stories. Think about the way the children were supported; the perspectives taken by the early childhood practitioners; the roles family members played in the stories; and how each child, practitioner, and family member grew. In Chapter 1 we discussed the various roles practitioners may play. Each role is distinctive yet critical in supporting the growth and development of *all* children in early childhood educational settings. However, developing a keen awareness of how these roles play out in supporting the child with special needs is very critical. Thus, we would like you to revisit these roles. They are:

- Broker of resources
- Locksmith opening doors to learning
- Architect designing unique opportunities for learning

- Bridge builder connecting the child with others
- Arbitrator of conflicts
- Champion of hope and inspiration

Each practitioner in the stories played a number of roles. Some of the roles played out more significantly in supporting the specific needs of the child than others. Create a profile of roles played by the practitioners in each of the stories. Think through both what the professionals did in each of the stories and how that may or may not fit into the roles described.

EXAMINING THE AFFECTIVE SIDE OF SERVING CHILDREN WITH SPECIAL NEEDS

In addition, other issues emerge as each of the stories is considered. First, let's examine how people handle their feelings about children with special needs and the special demands they create in a formal learning setting.

- How did you feel about each of the children, their families, and the professionals involved with each child?
- What evidence do you find that the professionals had various feelings about the children and the families when these particular challenges to learning were encountered?
- How did the families appear to feel about their encounters with the school or preschool settings? Why do you think they felt the way they did?
- As you review each of the cases, describe attitudes of the general education teachers toward the special education teachers. Were there any differences between the two groups on their views of the child?
- What evidence did you see regarding the parents' attitudes toward special education and general education, and why do you think that they might have these attitudes?

FOCUSING ON DEVELOPMENTALLY APPROPRIATE PRACTICES

The feelings and perceptions of adults either tend to motivate them into action or predispose them to choose actions to take in coping with the problems that they encounter. However, the skills and knowledge of the early childhood professional also contribute both to the choices that one considers and the competency with which one acts on those choices. Professionals who aspire to developmentally appropriate practice focus on the principles of age appropriateness, individual appropriateness, and social and cultural appropriateness. As such, they attempt to engage in the following practices:

- Focusing on the whole child
- Individualizing the program to suit particular children
- Recognizing the importance of child-initiated activity
- Valuing the significance of play as a vehicle of learning
- Creating flexible, stimulating classroom environments
- Implementing an integrated curriculum
- Emphasizing children's learning by doing
- Giving children choices about what and how they learn
- Continuously assessing individual children and the program as a whole
- Developing partnerships with parents (Kostelnik, Whiren, & Soderman, 1999)

Using the above information summarizing key areas related to developmentally appropriate practices, respond to the following questions:

- Which of the developmentally appropriate practices did the teachers in each of the classrooms use? How effective did these strategies appear to be?
- How did the teachers attempt to teach the whole child, focusing on the strengths as well as the special needs of the child?
- What strategies did the teachers use to integrate the child with special needs into the group setting?
- How did the teachers cope with the needs of the whole group of children and with the challenges of a child with special needs?
- To what extent were the parents involved in the planning of the instructional program of their children? How did this happen before the child had an IEP? What was the effect of the diagnosis of special needs and the development of an individualized plan for the child?
- How did the storytellers who were in a preschool setting contribute to the IEP, if they contributed?

FINDING COMMON THREADS

As you review each of the case studies in this book, look for common threads across the stories. This will help you to use these stories as guides to your own decisions as you encounter other children and their families.

- What do all the children have in common?
- Identify common characteristics among the families who were described. In what ways do you think this group of families might be a unique subset of families?
- Did you notice any common problems faced by the children's teachers?
- If you were asked to describe some professional approaches that looked promising for the early childhood educator in the general setting, what would they be?
- What pitfalls did teachers experience?

APPLYING WHAT YOU HAVE LEARNED:
THE STORY OF AMANDA

Now that you have considered the feelings of the people involved, developmentally appropriate practices in the classroom, and particular strategies that might be used with a child with special needs in an early childhood setting, it is time to apply what you understand to a new child. Her teacher in the private preschool program where she was enrolled tells the story of Amanda.

The Family

The home visit was very unusual. Most families are very inviting and hospitable to us. Amanda's family did not respond like the others. I found it hard to get in touch with them to arrange for the home visit, and they found great difficulty in scheduling a time when both parents would be available. When I did visit, I observed few possessions in the home, no books or personal touches, only the bare necessities, even though the father made a point of stating that he came from a wealthy family in another part of the country. He made it clear that he was a very powerful person and that there were not many people of his status here where he was temporarily assigned. I think his attitude contributed to the family's isolation in the local community.

During the home visit, the parents were very guarded and mistrustful. Though very well educated, they answered questions about Amanda's interests and development with one word or two. They acted as if they did not notice the child in front of them. There were no books or toys visible. The parents did not seem to recognize that Amanda had needs of her own. They seemed disconnected with the reality of Amanda.

This disconnection became more evident later in the schoolyear when it became cold. I told them that she needed a warm coat that fit her. They said her coat was new, but I could see that it was at least two sizes too small for her. All of her clothing was too small. Amanda was extremely obese in addition to being very tall for her age. I think they were in strong denial about her appearance as well as about her extreme behavior. I think they bought clothes for the small, docile child they wish they had. They made excuses for her outbursts and inappropriate actions instead of setting limits and following though with them.

Amanda had a lot of power and control in her family. Clearly she had more power than her mother, whom she hit repeatedly during my home visit until I intervened. From my observation, this family had little or no support on parenting. No one was there who could tell them that setting limits was okay and that children would survive crying. Nor was it evident that they desired help in child rearing. Amanda ate what she wanted to when she wanted to, which meant that she ate nearly all the time. At 3 years of age, she was still attached to a bottle when she went to bed at night.

After several conferences with me, the father did take Amanda to a pediatric dentist and a pediatrician. Her parents began to address the dental and dietary problems in January but remained resistant to information related to her learning difficulties and her socialization problems to the end. In fact, I was surprised that they even came back to my classroom after the winter break.

The Child

Amanda was a very large child, atypical for her age. She was at least a head taller than any other 3-year-old in the group and weighed about 60 pounds. Because she had been sucking on a bottle much too long, her teeth were really rotten. She was clearly motor- and language-delayed right from the beginning. She looked like she wasn't healthy, well kept, or cared for. Her hair was wispy and flyaway, uncombed and uncut. She wasn't always clean and did not have good hygiene. I wondered if her mom just couldn't get her to cooperate. Her defiant behavior and unkempt demeanor did not make her a particularly appealing child, though she smiled a lot.

Her physical presence was always noticeable. When she entered a group, it was as though the whole activity level changed. Her hands were always moving. She was grabbing people or material. She used a lot of two-handed, forceful pushing of others, with sudden, jerky movements. She treated people like things and did not appear to differentiate between how to treat people and animals and how to treat a puzzle or ball—and those she treated roughly.

Separation from her mother was really traumatic for her. At drop-off time she cried, was resistant to leaving the car, and did not appear to remember that she had been to school the day before. Just bringing her inside and up the stairs into the classroom was an ordeal, with her size and resistance. This behavior went on for weeks even though she appeared to enjoy the program once she got inside. She didn't appear to recognize me or the school. She did not appear to understand what was happening.

Amanda was very strong-willed and determined. She was very clear about what she wanted to do, and it seemed that she thought, "This is what I want to do, and this is what I'm going to do, and this is how I'm going to get your attention to help me!" She had a strong personality without the socialization skills or the understanding of limits. She had huge explosions whenever she was denied something.

Amanda had very little impulse control, and simple directions went right over her head. There was no rhyme or reason to her movements in the classroom. We could not predict her behavior or figure out her preferences even though we did time/event samples. Her walk was similar to that of a toddler, with a lot of sway, and she bumped into things all the time, even doors and large furniture. She could not move smoothly around the room. She had a very short attention span. She was rarely successful at manipulating materials successfully. She did not appear to understand how to play with simple toys.

Amanda communicated physically, using a lot of moans, groans, grunts, and pointing in addition to other hand motions. I got slapped a lot. It was not a gentle pat or the typical tugging or pulling young children frequently use to get attention; she was very forceful and rough. Her nails were unclipped, so when she grabbed she would scratch as well. She hurt people to get what she wanted or to get their attention. Amanda was unsocialized, like a wild child. Large group was very complicated for her to participate in; she had difficulty sitting long enough for us to interest her. Even turning pages in a book was very difficult for her. She had trouble turning the pages of a book without ripping the pages or having them fall out. It took one-to-one supervision, with modeling and support, for her to be successful at this. She was very sensory-motivated, but she didn't understand the limits; because she would mouth objects, we had to be careful that she did not ingest things.

Other children reacted to Amanda with fear. Some of the most sophisticated children treated her with a sort of disdain. Mostly they left an area when she entered it or they called out for help. It really startled me when children got to the point of calling for help when they noticed that she might come over to the area where they were playing. For the children, it was total rejection. Even though she hit them hard enough to make them cry, they did not hit her back. They seemed to figure out that it would not matter whatever they did.

Strategies Attempted

We did a lot of reflecting on our strategies and wondered if her large size was throwing us. Were we expecting more of her than what was appropriate? We used a lot of redirecting and modeling of appropriate behaviors. When she really hurt someone, she had time away from the group until she could settle down. She was very resistant and just wanted to go back to doing her own thing. I am not sure if she ever understood what was happening, and after a while we just used strategies to enable all of us to survive.

For her the limits had to be very clear, with few options. When it was time to go inside and she did not want to, she could either walk in by herself or adults would help her. And it took two adults to follow through because she was such a large child.

On Monday she was shadowed [*followed closely by one adult from area to area*], and the rest of the week she was zoned [*adults in various sectors of the room were alert to her movement in the area and took over close supervision*]. These strategies were necessary for keeping people safe. Prevention of inappropriate behavior was the most successful strategy.

Another strategy was to help her to observe the results of her actions and the effects they had on other people (and things) and to observe how to make things better. I don't think she understood natural consequences or logical consequences. Most of the time we were not successful. Praise didn't work either. She just didn't connect.

Amanda was a puzzling child when she came, and she was still a puzzling child when she left. I never really understood her developmental problems, and with parents so completely in denial, there was no practical support from them. Unfortunately, there was never an opportunity to get any formal assessment that might have helped clarify some of her issues. In dealing with a child and family like this, it is important to have a colleague or an administrator with whom you can ask the hard questions, to examine your own biases. You have to work out which is the "gut" response and which the intellectual response. You have to trust your own knowledge base of what is typical development and what is atypical; and when things don't match up, you have to be honest with the parents. As hard and as uncomfortable and as threatening as that may be, it is very important to bring the parents' attention to your collection of documented, organized observations. It can't be off the cuff.

In reflecting on an experience such as mine with Amanda, I think that you have to look at the small victories. Amanda did make some progress. She eventually became less aggressive; her parents had her dental problems treated; she was cleaner and neater when she left the program.

DISCUSSING WHAT YOU HAVE LEARNED

1. Now that you know a little bit about Amanda, what would you do to support her if she were to enroll in your program?
2. What questions would you have about her?
3. How would you develop strategies for supporting her learning?
4. How would you approach her family?
5. What family assets might you use to support Amanda's learning and growth in the classroom?

FINAL THOUGHTS

Like any child in a classroom, children with special needs are learners, unique in their own special way. Children with special needs have assets as well as characteristics that challenge parents and teachers who provide them with opportunities for growth and development. They also learn in the context of families that are unique in structure, culture, and expectations. Furthermore, the neighborhoods and communities in which families reside vary in accessibility and resources. Understanding all these variables among children with special needs is essential as you strive to support *all* children in your early childhood educational setting. The authors of this book hope that the lessons you have learned from the children, teachers, and parents cited in this book will help you in this endeavor.

REFERENCE

Kostelnik, M. J., Whiren, A. P., & Soderman, A. K. (1999). *Developmentally appropriate curriculum: Best practices in early childhood education.* Upper Saddle River, NJ: Merrill.

A P P E N D I X   A

Individual Education Program Process

The Individual Education Program (IEP) emerged through federal legislation—the Education of the Handicapped Act (EHA) in 1975 and later the Individuals with Disabilities Education Act (IDEA)—for the education of special needs children and youth. The purpose of the IEP is to ensure (1) the involvement and progress of each child with a disability in the general curriculum, (2) the involvement of parents and students, and general education and special education personnel, in supporting the student's educational needs, and (3) the preparation of students with disabilities for employment and other postschool activities.

You may encounter a family with a child who has an IEP or an Individual Family Plan of Service (IFPS). The most recent legislation has included special provisions for children from birth to age 3. For more information on your state, visit the National Information Center for Children and Youth with Disabilities (NICHY) Website (www.nichy.org). For children from birth to age 3 who are identified as having special needs, the IFSP is developed with the family, an identified coordinator, and other professionals who are able to provide the needed services. The IFSP describes the child's development levels and details family information, the major child and family outcomes expected to be achieved, the services the child will be receiving, when and where the child will receive services, and the steps to support the child's transition into another program. The family may talk to you about the child's IFSP or you may be contacted by the child's IFSP coordinator.

A more common occurrence is to be invited to be a part of a child's IEP. The next sections describe what you might experience as an invited member at an IEP meeting and elements in an IEP document.

THE IEP DOCUMENT

The IEP is a plan developed at least once a year, with much the same components as the IFSP. It is comprised of annual goals, short-term objectives or benchmarks of progress, how and when the objectives will be measured, current assessment of the child's performance, and services that the child will receive.

THE IEP MEETING

Advance Preparation

The IEP coordinator ensures that the results of the assessments are completed and ready for review at the meeting. There may be some informal meetings prior to the IEP among various individuals to discuss plausible goals and objectives for the child as the next steps. Professionals are not to bring their written goals and objectives with the expectation that parents will sign the form. Having parental input into the creation of goals and objectives is a core component of the IEP. Parents may invite others whom they feel might contribute to the construction of the IEP.

Getting Started: Creating Shared Visions and Expectations

The IEP coordinator will greet the participants and introduce everyone. If this is the first time for the parents, the coordinator may spend a few minutes describing the process and the parents' rights regarding participaton in the meeting. If not, an annual update and review of the current IEP will be conducted.

Reviewing Evaluations on the Level of Performance

Parents receive written copies of evaluations of present levels of educational performance, including descriptions of how the child's disability affects his or her involvement in the general curriculum and the child's participation in appropriate activities. The evaluation findings are summarized, including the child's strengths, gifts, abilities, and needs. The implications for the child's progress in the general curriculum and extracurricular activities are discussed. Once members reach a consensus about the child's exceptionality and current levels of performance, the IEP process continues.

Developing Goals and Objectives

Usually parents come to the meeting with some goals in mind that they think their child can and should achieve. Specialists and other IEP team members may also come prepared with drafted goals based on observations of the child's performance or progress and on their assessment of the child's current needs. These goals and objectives are frequently prioritized. For example, independent use of the toilet is frequently prioritized higher on the list than is grooming if both are being considered for a young child.

During this part of the meeting, the parents and others clarify responsibilities for teaching specific objectives. The team may be all working toward a specific objective (e.g., toilet training). In other instances, the speech therapist may take the lead in working on simple words for making requests, while the others on the team reinforces the child's performance.

The goals set are not guaranteed to be met; they are simply goals and objectives to be worked toward. Plans can be developed for strategies that might lead to successful achievement of the goals. The extended day or extended school year during which services would be provided to support the child's learning could be discussed.

The means for reporting progress to the parents are also agreed on at the meeting. Waivers for district or classroom tests may be arranged.

Sharing Resources, Priorities, and Concerns

The services and supports needed to achieve the goals and objectives are discussed. Services (speech, occupational, physical, or mental health therapy) are prioritized. Parents contribute their ideas about the priorities they would place on the necessary resources that would best support their child's needs.

Determining Placement and Other Services

The placement options and the strengths and weaknesses of each option are reviewed. In general, the team strives to include the child with his or her typically developing peers. The degree to which the child can participate in the general school curriculum should be agreed on, and the necessary supports to enable the child to be successful in that environment should be identified. Parents should be encouraged to visit the program or classroom where the child will potentially be placed. Information about qualifications of the personnel and the type of programming provided in that setting could also be presented to the parents.

Concluding the Meeting

The IEP coordinator summarizes the decisions that were made and the areas of disagreement, if any. If the parents concur with the plans designed at the meeting, they will sign the IEP form along with the other participants.

The coordinator reviews the responsibilities for follow-up as well as how ongoing communication among those present will be conducted as identified by Turnbull, Turnbull, Shank, and Leal (1999).

REFERENCE

Turnbull, A., Turnbull, R., Shank, M., & Leal, D. (1999). *Exceptional lives: Special education in today's schools.* Upper Saddle River, NJ: Prentice Hall.

Contents of an Individual Education Program for Young Children

The IEP form may vary from one school district to another, but there are some common components required by law.

1. Describe the elementary school–age child's level of educational performance or, in the case of a preschool-age child, describe how the disability affects participation in appropriate activities. The following five areas will be considered in the IEP process, per the Individuals with Disabilities Education Act (IDEA):
   Physical abilities
   Communication abilities
   Thinking (cognitive) abilities
   Social and emotional behavior
   Developmental or educational growth
   Any other areas specific to the child
2. *Strengths.* Look at the whole child's gifts, talents, and abilities
   Example: Jake can put on his own shoes
3. *Needs.* Be specific in thinking about what the child needs in order to benefit from the education schools offer.
   Example: Cary needs to develop eye contact with the person with whom she is speaking.
4. *Annual goals.* What would you like your child to be able to do a year from now? The goals should be individualized and be connected to the needs. The goal is an activity; it describes what the child will do and the conditions under which the child will do it.

      Example: Luke will use picture-symbols to communicate what he wants to do during free time.

5. *Short-Term Objectives.* Define the steps the child will take to reach his or her goal. Objectives must be observable and measurable. Included are how objectives will be measured and the time line for achieving them.

      Example: Kyle will go to and come back from the music room with his peers; measured by teacher observation; by March 1, 2001.

6. *Related services and supplementary aids and services.* State services and program modifications or supports that will be provided for the child so that he or she can advance toward the annual goals, be involved and progress in the general curriculum and participate in extracurricular activities, and be educated and participate with other children with disabilities and children without disabilities.

7. *Placement.* Determine placement after giving consideration to the child's strengths and needs, the goals, and related services needed and characteristics of these services.

8. *Time and place.* Determine the projected date for the beginning of the services and modifications, as well as the anticipated frequency, location, and duration of the services and modifications.

9. *Signatures.* Procure the signatures of parents, the student if a participant, teachers, and others who have been asked by the parents to participate in the IEP.

      (Adapted from http://www.kidstogether.org)

Index

About the Authors

Marjorie J. Kostelnik, Ph.D., is dean of the College of Human Resources and Family Sciences at the University of Nebraska. Beginning as a Head Start teacher, she has worked directly with children and families for 20 years in a variety of early childhood settings. She includes among her areas of teaching and scholarship child socialization and developmentally appropriate practices with young children. Dr. Kostelnik is widely published in the field of early childhood education and has presented to audiences worldwide. She served NAEYC (the National Association for Early Childhood Education) as vice president from 1994–1998 and was recently honored with the Michigan Council of Cooperative Nurseries Lifetime Achievement Award. She earned her doctorate in Human Development and Family Studies from the Pennsylvania State University.

Esther Onaga is associate professor of family and child ecology at Michigan State University, where she teaches courses in community services, families of children with disabilities, program development and design, and research methods. She uses service learning with a summer study in Hawaii to teach about human diversity. Her current research involves the study of inclusion in recreation and leisure activities and the study of clubhouses to support people with psychiatric disabilities. She helped establish the Coalition for Community Living, a national organization that supports programs providing residential and employment supports for people with psychiatric disabilities. She holds a Ph.D. in ecological/community psychology from Michigan State University and a B.Ed. and M.Ed. in special education from the University of Hawaii.

Barbara Rohde is currently associate supervisor of the Child Development Laboratories, Michigan State University, which serve 300 children from 3 months to 6 years old, including many special needs children. She has been an early childhood educator for 34 years, teaching school-age children, preschoolers, and adults. She has taught courses at Michigan State University and Central Michigan University. She administered a program for at-risk preschoolers serving families in the mid-Michigan area. She supports best practices in classrooms throughout the state of Michigan through her workshops and consulting. Her published writing includes chapters in *Teaching Young Children Using Themes and Developmentally Appropriate Curriculum: Best Practices for Early Childhood Education.*

Alice Whiren is a professor in the Department of Family and Child Ecology at Michigan State University. She has been a teacher in public school preschools, an assistant director of Head Start, and a supervisor of the Child Development Laboratories at Michigan State University and has published in the areas of guidance and curriculum in early childhood. She has been an advocate for the inclusion of children with special needs into programs designed primarily for typically developing children since 1964, when she first had a child with Down syndrome in her preschool classroom. She is also the parent of two children who have special needs.